D1317673

Exploring Winter

EXPLORING WINTER

written and illustrated by

Sandra Markle

Atheneum | *New York*

For Bob and Dorothy Haldeman,
my parents,
who first showed me the fun
of exploring every season.

Atheneum
Macmillan Publishing Company
866 Third Avenue, New York, NY 10022
Collier Macmillan Canada, Inc.
Printed in the United States of America
First Edition
3 5 7 9 11 13 15 17 19 20 18 16 14 12 10 8 6 4

Library of Congress Cataloging in Publication Data
Markle, Sandra. Exploring winter.
Includes index.
SUMMARY: A collection of winter-time activities which include stories and facts about animals, explorers, and survival, instructions for building a snow shelter and making instruments to measure the weather, as well as games, riddles, and puzzles.
1. Winter—Juvenile literature. [1. Winter. 2. Amusements] I. Title.
QH81.M267 1984 574.5'43 84-3049
ISBN 0-689-31065-X

CONTENTS

IS IT WINTER YET?

IS IT winter yet? Is it dark before you get done with supper and dark when you get up in the morning? When you go outside, do you get red cheeks, a runny nose, numb toes?

Winter comes out in a fog when you talk. It's naked branches, rock salt on the sidewalks, needles of ice slicing through the glow of streetlights and headlights. Winter is crunchy sounds when you walk, wet wool, puddles leaking around your boots on the clean hall floor. It's your jacket zipper catching the front of your shirt and staying stuck no matter how you try to wiggle it loose.

Winter is crackling fires, first run shows on TV, hot cocoa with marshmallows melting on top. It's going outside without getting mosquito bites and without worrying about bears. Sometimes winter is dull, slippery, gray, boring.

Is it winter yet? Almost? Then this book is for you.

It has icy investigations and instructions for building your own snow shelter. There are stories about how animals make it through winter and tales of famous Arctic and Antarctic explorers. It has survival facts and hints for exploring this frosty frontier on your own. There are directions for encouraging plants to bloom early and instructions for making weather instruments to do your own forecasting. You can make snow snakes and an Eskimo buzzer. There are games to play, riddles to laugh at, and puzzlers to think about. Not to mention indoor explorations for times when it's too awful to go outside.

This book is guaranteed to bring out that secret desire to become an explorer that lurks inside of you. Once you start, you definitely won't want to curl up and hibernate.

Is it winter yet? Get ready. Winter is too exciting to miss.

1. WINTER IS COMING

Looking for Signs

CAN YOU tell that winter is coming? In parts of the country where there are distinct seasons, the approach of winter is signaled by leaves changing color, birds heading south, and animals preparing to survive the hard months ahead. But even where winter doesn't make such a dramatic entrance, there are two sure-fire signs that forecast the arrival of the season:

1) The constellations that you see in the nighttime sky begin to change.
2. The hours of daylight become increasingly shorter.

Both of these signs show you that winter is really a matter of where you (and Spaceship Earth) are on that annual jaunt around the sun. The sun has a lot to do with it being winter or some other season.

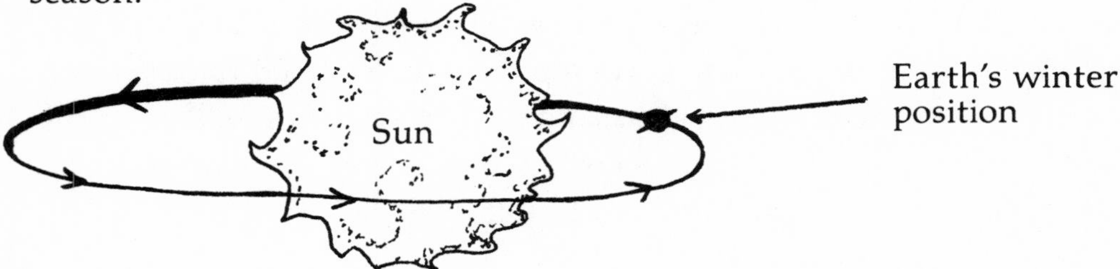

The sun is a ball of exploding gas estimated to be about 5,500°C. (10,000°F.) at its surface. Energy in the form of heat, visible light, ultraviolet light (the type of radiation that gives you a sunburn), radio waves and X rays shoot out from the sun in a steady stream. The length of day and how warm it is depends on how much solar energy reaches the earth.

So why does the earth receive more sunlight during some seasons than at others? Is the earth farther from the sun in the winter?

No. Surprisingly, the earth is closer to the sun in the winter than it is in the summer.

Winter and the amount of sunlight reaching the earth is entirely a matter of tilt.

Tilt

(Or shedding some light on the reason for Winter)

THE EARTH has an imaginary axis running through its North and South Poles. During the winter months for the northern hemisphere (half of the earth), the area where the United States is located points away from the sun. The sun's rays strike at a slant, and slanted rays carry less energy than rays hitting the earth directly.

You can see how much less energy slanted winter rays supply by following the steps of this investigation. You'll need two pieces of newspaper, a magnifying glass, and a quart jar full of water. Do this on a sunny day. Work on a sidewalk or a driveway away from dry grass or anything else that might catch fire.

Spread out one sheet of newspaper. Hold the magnifying glass over the paper. Tip the glass so the spot of light is about the size of a quarter and very bright. Hold your hand steady. Soon the paper will begin to smoke, and then it will burst into flames. Dump the water on the fire to put it out.

RIDDLE

What did the Eskimo say after he finished building his igloo?

ANSWER: Ours is an ice (a nice) house.

Spread out the second sheet of paper. Hold the magnifying glass so the spot of light is the size of a softball. Now, the rays are striking the paper at an angle. Because the light rays are spreading out, there is less heat energy focused on the paper. The paper may eventually get hot enough to burn, but it will take a lot longer for this to happen.

Winter is also colder because there are fewer hours when the sunlight reaches the northern hemisphere to provide warmth.

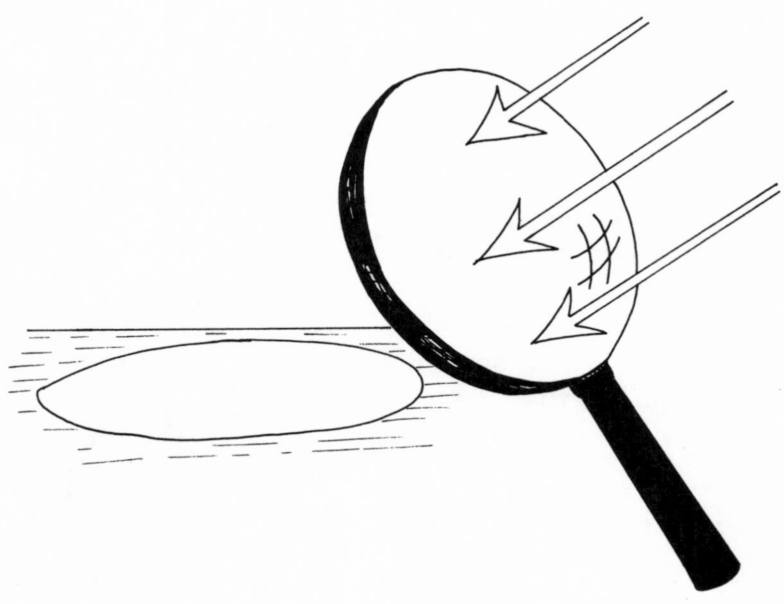

Getting an Angle on the Angle

JUST HOW MUCH does the temperature change as the angle of sunlight reaching the earth changes? You can use your shadow to find out.

When the weather prediction is for sunny and clear, place a thermometer on a driveway or a sidewalk at nine o'clock in the morning. Wait five minutes. Then record the temperature.

Now comes the tricky part. Place one foot on either side of the thermometer and have a friend outline your shadow with chalk.

Repeat this process exactly at noon and again at three o'clock. Stand in the same spot each time. For the most interesting results, have your friend outline each shadow in a different color.

The lower the angle of light, the longer your shadow will be. When was your shadow longest? Shortest? At what time was the temperature reading highest? Lowest?

Imagine what the earth's weather would be like if the earth was not tipped as it orbits the sun. How would such a change affect the frozen poles? Would there be a seasonal change in the length of daylight as there is now?

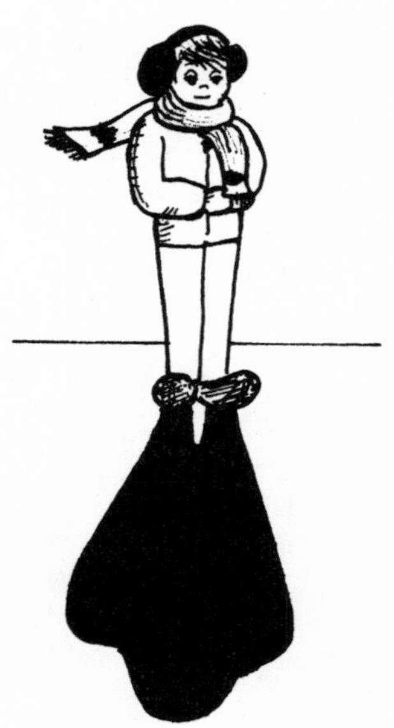

Remember, the equator always receives direct sunlight. Day and night at the equator are each twelve hours long.

PUZZLER

It's 5°C. (40°F.) in Sidney, Australia, and the forecast for tomorrow is even colder. Is it January, March, or June?

(See page 13.)

When Is Winter?

WINTER in the northern hemisphere officially begins on December 21. This day is called the *winter solstice.* It is the day when the North Pole of the earth is tipped farthest from the sun. It is also the day with the fewest daylight hours.

Winter lasts eighty-nine days and one hour according to astronomers, people who study the heavens. March 21 is officially the last day of winter.

In the southern hemisphere, June 21 marks the beginning of winter. This is the day when the South Pole is tipped farthest from the sun. The long winter months of July, August and September are marked by shorter periods of sunlight and cold, winter storms.

IT'S WAR!

In Eskimo villages, the people don't leave what winter will be like to chance. They hold a contest each fall to forecast the coming winter weather.

The ducks (anyone born during a summer month) line up on one side, and the ptarmigans (anyone born during a winter month) line up facing them. A sealskin rope is stretched between the two teams, and the tug of war begins.

If the ducks win, winter will be fair and mild. If the ptarmigans win, better bundle up.

Check your friends' birthdays and set up a tug of war of your own to predict the coming winter.

Weird Winters

RECORD EARLY and late snowfalls may be a result of storms on the sun. These storms cause solar flares to erupt from the sun's surface with the force of a billion hydrogen bombs. If the earth wasn't protected by a strong magnetic field and an atmosphere, this radiation could destroy all life. Instead, the weather goes crazy.

Meteorologists, people who study the weather, believe that volcanic eruptions and other natural events also cause weird weather.

Minutes after Mount Saint Helens erupted on May 18, 1980, a terrible ash storm, supercharged with static electricity hurled lightning at Glenoma, Washington twenty miles away. Much of the state of Washington was coated with ash, and the sky remained as dark as night for days.

In 1815, Mount Tambora on a small Indonesian island suddenly erupted. The volcano blew tons of ash and smoke into the atmosphere. Houses and fields on the island of Java several hundred miles away were covered by ash. Even worse was the effect this eruption had on the weather.

The eastern United States had frosts in May, a heavy snow in June, and terrible rainstorms in July and August.

The fall harvest was so bad world-wide that by winter many people were starving.

Volcanic ash in the atmosphere decreases the amount of

sunlight that can filter through to the earth. This general cooling effect, plus added dust for water drops to form around, causes increased rainfalls and snowfalls.

PUZZLER ANSWER

It's June. South America, South Africa and Australia are tipped away from the sun when it's summer in the United States.

Jet Stream

THE JET STREAM is a very high, fast-moving current of air blowing from west to east across the United States. Pilots have to pay attention to the location of this wind because flying against the stream slows them down. Even more important is the effect the jet stream has on the weather.

Normally, this wind acts as a weather barrier, holding cold Arctic storms to the North. During the winter of 1976-77, a slipped jet stream temporarily made winter weird for much of the United States.

PUZZLER

On the first day of winter, does the sun ever rise at the North Pole? (See page 14.)

Parts of the South had record cold temperatures, heavy snows and ice storms. Normally cold states of the northern plains were shielded from the Arctic gales. Warm tropical air moved up, bringing record high temperatures to that northern area.

Animals Get Ready for Winter

ANIMALS meet the challenge of winter in different ways. Some grow warmer coats, make their home weatherproof and find food where they can. Some migrate—travel to where it's warmer. Others curl up where it's warm and dry to sleep the long, dark winter days away.

When an animal hibernates, the heart rate and breathing rate is greatly reduced. All of the body processes are slowed so much that the animal can live off the food stored within its body. Not all winter sleepers, however, are hibernating. These nappers wake up and hunt for food whenever the weather warms up.

RIDDLE

What's the difference between the North Pole and the South Pole?

ANSWER: The whole world

PUZZLER ANSWER

No. On December 21 (the winter solstice) the North Pole is pointed away from the sun for the entire twenty-four hour rotation. On the first day of summer, the North Pole is aimed at the sun. The sun never sets on that day.

Chipmunks

CHIPMUNKS dig deep underground tunnels for their winter home. At the end of this tunnel, a room is hollowed out and filled with nuts and seeds. Then the chipmunk builds a bed of grass and leaves on top of its food supply. Curled up in a tight ball, the chipmunk sleeps most of the winter, waking up from time to time to eat and peek outside.

Bats

SOME KINDS of bats fly south for the winter. But most insect-eating bats stay in the north, returning to the same cave every year. Thousands and even millions of bats may hibernate together, hanging upside down from nooks and cracks in the ceiling. Asleep, the bat's body temperature lowers until it is barely higher than the air temperature. That is why it is important that the bats' winter home be deep enough that the air temperature remains above freezing all winter long.

Squirrels

SOME SQUIRRELS nest in hollow trees, but most live in nests they build themselves. If you see a bundle of leaves nestled among high branches of a bare tree, it's probably a squirrel's home. A squirrel sleeps the cold winter months away wrapped up in its bushy tail. From time to time on warm, sunny days, the squirrel wakes up and slips out to look for the nuts it buried just for these mid-winter snacks. But squirrels don't recover all the nuts they tuck away each year. What do you think happens to the ones the squirrels don't dig up?

Bird Nap

THE NORTH AMERICAN poorwill is the only bird known to hibernate. Sleeping poorwills have been spotted in the foothills of the Sierra Nevada Mountains. Snuggled into rock crevices, the poorwills are not bothered by bad weather.

Skunks

SKUNKS begin to eat more as winter approaches. They stuff themselves on insects, berries, grain, nuts, frogs, and snakes. Then when the weather turns cold, the skunks dig burrows.

Because they want a dry as well as a warm spot to sleep, skunks often burrow under houses or barns. Male skunks retire alone. Female skunks room together. Twelve or more females may spend the winter in the burrow. This is about as sociable as a skunk ever gets. Of course, no one is awake to enjoy the company.

Snakes

SNAKES, like turtles and lizards, are reptiles. Reptiles are cold-blooded, which means their bodies don't provide heat for them. As the weather gets colder, they crawl into caves, crevices in rocks, hollow logs or animal burrows to hibernate. Sometimes snakes will curl up

together with as many as a hundred snakes forming a tight ball. They do this to share space, not to keep warm.

Turtles

TURTLES have a shell to cover at least part of their body, and in winter they tuck exposed body parts inside this built-in shelter. Turtles that live in water usually dig into the pond bottom. While hibernating, their body functions slow down so much that the air stored in the turtles' lungs plus what little oxygen can be absorbed from the water is enough. Turtles that live on land move into empty animal burrows or dig a burrow of their own. In colder areas, turtles may dig a winter home as much as four feet deep to be able to sleep below the frost line.

Frogs

FROGS, like salamanders and toads, are amphibians, which means they live part of their life in the water and part on land. They are cold-blooded and so escape the cold winter months by hibernating. Some frogs dig into pond bottoms, others burrow deep into the ground. Completely buried, frogs are able to absorb enough oxygen directly through their skin to survive.

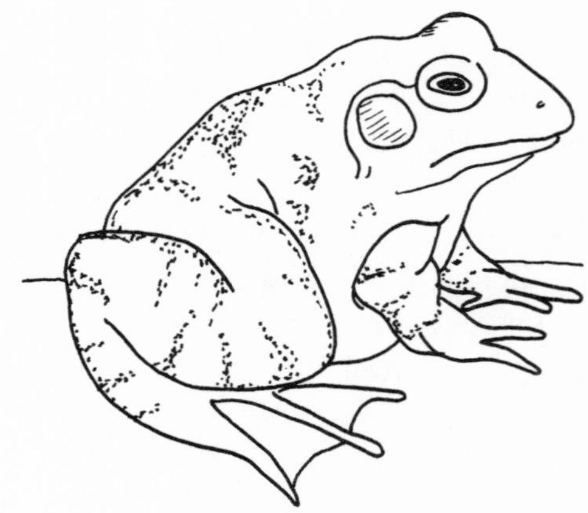

Fish

WHEN ICE covers lakes, the water becomes stale. There is less oxygen to breathe, and most fish sink to the bottom. They remain quiet but awake. Carp, however, flap their tails to cover themselves with mud and go to sleep. Insulated against the cold, the carp hibernate until the surface thaws and the oxygen level of the water improves.

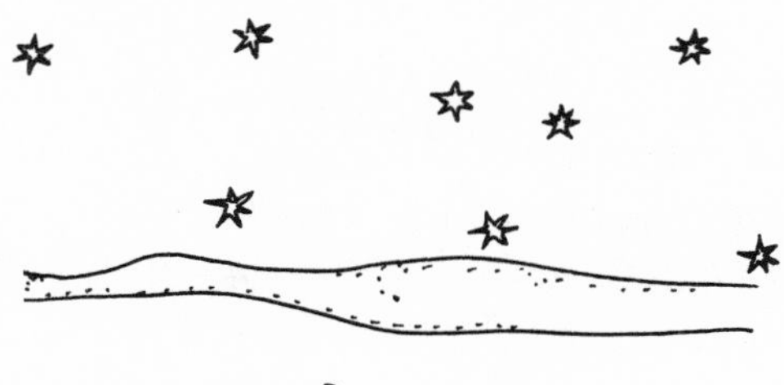

RIDDLE

Why did the bat hibernate in the chandelier?

ANSWER: Because it's a light sleeper

FROZEN FISH

Arctic graylings (related to trout) live off the coast of Alaska and northern Canada. These fish allow themselves to become trapped in solid ice. Suspended in their cold bed, the fish hibernate during the winter months.

Bears

BEARS spend spring, summer and fall eating. A bear can run thirty miles per hour to catch small game and can overturn rocks or boulders while searching for food. They are *omnivorous,* which means they will eat just about anything.

After three seasons of stuffing itself, a bear is ready for a long winter's nap. (Bears sleep rather than hibernate). Bears will sleep in a cave, under a barn, or on the north side of a hill where drifts will provide cover.

While female bears are sleeping, their cubs are born. The tiny naked babies press into their mother's fur and nurse. By spring, the cubs have a nice coat of fur and are ready to join their mother in a long feast. Father bears remain on their own.

Have the flocks of birds heading south already gone? Have the nappers and hibernators tucked themselves away? Are the hours of daylight getting shorter? Is the weather colder?

GREAT!

Winter is here.

Don't wait another minute to get started.

2. COOL INVESTI- GATIONS

YOU CAN DO all the investigations in this book on your own or for even more fun you can share the adventures with friends. To make *Exploring Winter* more challenging, from now on all riddle answers will be in pigpen cipher. So read *Secret Code* carefully. Then make a copy of the code or memorize it and be prepared. You might also want to use this code to share expedition secrets with your friends.

Secret Code

THE PIGPEN CIPHER (also called the Freemason's cipher) is perfect for secret messages. Ciphers replace letters with symbols. This code is fast to use and easy to remember with a little practice. The pigpen cipher was developed over a hundred years ago during the Civil War. Northern prisoners in Confederate prisons used it to communicate with friends on the outside.

In this code, it's the position that counts. The word *winter* looks like this in cipher:

For punctuation marks, use the real thing.

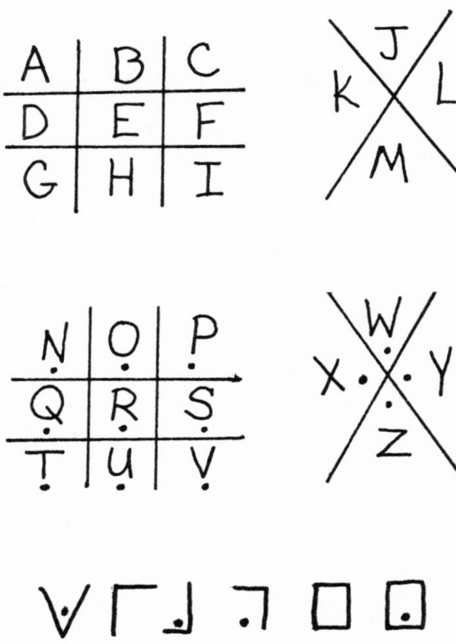

Here is a little more practice. Encode this: What bank has no money? Decode this:

You can also find the answers on page 154.

How Cold Is Cold?

ACTUALLY, any question of temperature has to start with heat energy. Cold is simply the lack of heat energy.

Everything is made up of tiny particles called atoms and atom groups called molecules. The arrangement of these particles and the amount of space between them determines whether the matter is a solid, a liquid or a gas.

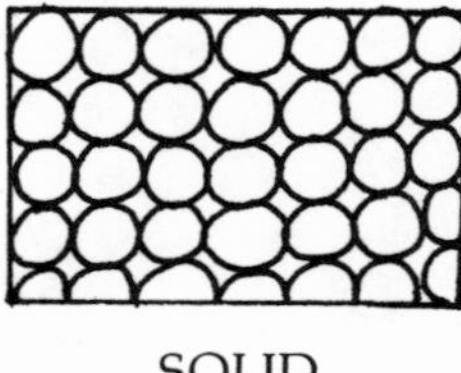

SOLID

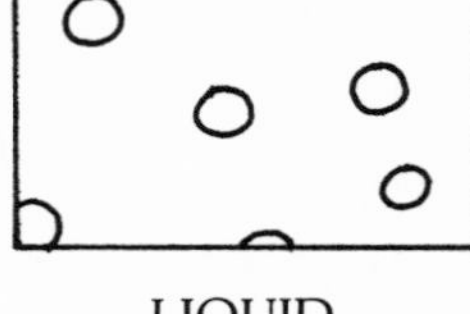

LIQUID

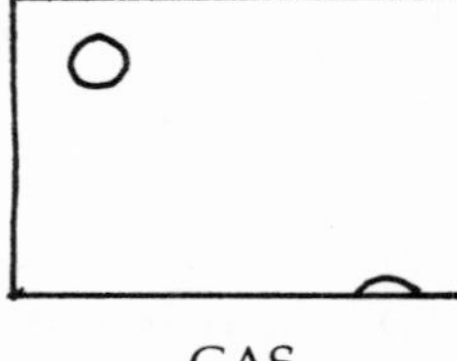

GAS

When heat energy is supplied, the atoms or molecules begin to move faster. The particles in a solid speed up and the back-and-forth motion causes the substance to expand. As molecules spread out, the solid changes to a liquid and then to a gas.

Temperature is how much or how little heat is present. It is measured in degrees.

Galileo Galilei was the first person to measure heat. In 1593, he built an instrument called a *thermoscope*. This was simply a narrow glass tube filled with liquid. It could show temperature changes, but it couldn't accurately measure temperatures. Air molecules moved freely in the open tube and pressed on the liquid, preventing it from expanding completely.

In 1714, Gabriel Daniel Fahrenheit invented the first accurate thermometer. He used a sealed glass tube into which mercury was injected. All the air molecules were removed (forming a vacuum) so they wouldn't interfere. The Fahrenheit (F.) scale was based on the lowest temperature possible for a mixture of salt and water, and at the opposite extreme the blood temperature of humans.

Anders Celsius created his own measurement scale (Celsius or Centigrade, C.) in 1742. This scale was developed mainly to measure the high melting temperatures of metals. Today, it is more widely used than the Fahrenheit scale.

PUZZLER

Why are strips of tar placed between slabs of concrete in a sidewalk? (See page 27.)

Feeling Cold

YOU'LL NEED three bowls (all the same size and big enough to stick your hand into). Fill one bowl with hot water and another with cold water. Place the third bowl between these two, and fill it with lukewarm water.

Now, put one hand in the hot water and the other hand in the cold water. Hold your hands in the bowls for one minute. Then plunge both hands into the middle bowl.

To the hand that was chilled, the water will feel warm. To the hand that was heated, the water will feel cool. The different sensations were determined by whether heat energy was being transferred to or conducted away your skin.

Take It Away

WHEN HEAT ENERGY moves from one atom or molecule to another, the transfer is called *conduction*. Some materials are good conductors, which means they let heat energy move through them easily. You can't see the energy transfer, but you can prove that conduction is happening.

Collect some old candle wax, a candle in a holder, matches, aluminum foil, a metal coat hanger, a yardstick, and a stack of books.

Roll the wax in your hand to

form four small balls. Press these wax balls onto the bottom of the hanger, spacing them from the middle to one end.

Use the books and the yardstick to suspend the hanger. The bare end of the hanger should be right over the candle flame when the candle is lit. Be careful to keep the candle flame away from the books! Place a piece of foil under the hanger to catch the falling wax balls.

Light the candle and check the time. How long does it take heat to reach the first wax ball and make it drop off? How can you tell that heat is being conducted through the wire from the candle flame?

PUZZLER ANSWER

The tar strips give the concrete slabs room to expand without being squeezed so tightly together that they crack.

PUZZLER

In the Depression (a time when many people were out of work), people often couldn't afford a lot of winter clothes. Some people stuffed newspaper into their shoes and pockets to keep warm. Why did newspaper help? (See page 29.)

CONDUCTORS AT A GLANCE

GOOD	Steel, Aluminum, Silver, Copper, Water, Gold

POOR	Wood, Wool, Air, Styrofoam, Some rubber, Some plastics

Good Conductors—Poor Conductors

IF YOU could check a lot of different substances, you would discover that the best conductors are metal. Did you ever put a spoon in a bowl of hot soup and suddenly find the handle too hot to touch?

Water is another super heat conductor. In the summer, your body pours sweat onto your skin. This moisture (a mixture of water, salt, and body wastes) conducts heat away and cools you.

In the winter, sweating and getting wet can be dangerous, carrying away needed body heat.

To stay warm, you need poor conductors around you. Wood, wool and air are such poor conductors that they've been named insulators.

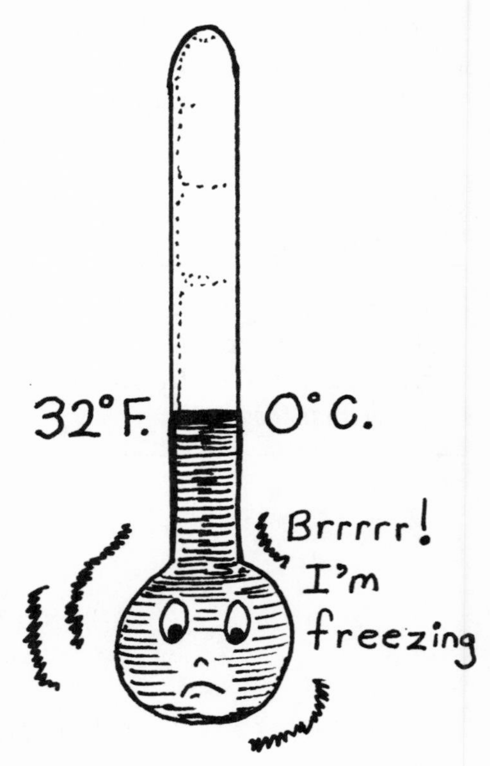

WEATHER TRIVIA

World's lowest temperature: -87°C.(-125°F.), August 25, 1958 in Vostok, Antarctica. Coldest U.S. temperature: -62°C.(-80°F.), January 23, 1971 in Prospect Creek, Alaska.

PUZZLER ANSWER

The newspaper acted as insulation, helping to trap body heat.

Brrrrrrr!

AIR IS a terrible conductor of heat, but when you start air moving, you have wind. Wind will carry heat away in a hurry.

The thermometer says that the temperature outside is -6°C. (23°F.), but with the wind blowing 32 kmph (20 mph), it feels like -67°C. (-9°F.). Try this experiment to see just how chilling the wind can be. You'll need two thermometers, a magazine and a clock with a second hand.

Put the two thermometers about 3 meters (10 feet) apart. Make sure that neither is in the sun, a draft, or close to an air vent. Check the temperature of each thermometer and write it down.

Rapidly fan one thermometer for two full minutes. Then compare the two thermometers again. The reading on the one you fanned will be lower. How much lower is it?

Obviously, if you're going to explore outside in winter, you're going to have to work at keeping warm. Water (in the form of rain, snow, ice, and your own sweat) and wind will be working against you.

Wind Chill Factor Chart

Calm Air Temperature
C°(F°)

Windspeed in Kilometers (Miles) per hour	2 (35)	-1 (30)	-3 (25)	-6 (20)	-9 (15)	-12 (10)	-15 (5)	-17 (0)	-20 (-5)	-23 (-10)
8 (5)	.5 (33)	-2 (33)	-6 (21)	-8 (16)	-11 (12)	-14 (7)	-17 (1)	-21- (-6)	-24 (-11)	-26 (-15)
16 (10)	-6 (21)	-8 (16)	-13 (9)	-17 (2)	-19 (-2)	-23 (-9)	-26 (-15)	-30 (-22)	-33 (-27)	-35 (-31)
24 (15)	-9 (16)	-11 (11)	-17 (1)	-21 (-6)	-24 (-11)	-28 (-18)	-32 (-25)	-36 (-33)	-40 (-40)	-43 (-45)
32 (20)	-11 (12)	-16 (3)	-20 (-4)	-23 (-9)	-27 (-17)	-31 (-24)	-36 (-32)	-40 (-40)	-43 (-46)	-47 (-52)
40 (25)	-14 (7)	-18 (0)	-21 (-7)	-26 (-15)	-30 (-22)	-34 (-29)	-38 (-37)	-42 (-45)	-47 (-52)	-50 (-58)
48 (30)	-15 (5)	-18 (-2)	-24 (-11)	-28 (-18)	-32 (-26)	-36 (-33)	-41 (-41)	-45 (-49)	-49 (-56)	-53 -(63)

READ THE chart by putting one index finger on the wind speed and the other on the calm air temperature. Bring your two fingers together. The point where they meet shows the temperature as it feels with the wind chill factor.

Built-In Furnace

WHEN YOU START thinking about how to keep warm, remember this. Unlike snakes, frogs, fish and worms, you are warm-blooded. Being warm-blooded means that your body changes the food that you eat into heat energy. You have a built-in furnace.

So how good a heat producer are you?

Check the temperature on a thermometer and write it down. Put the thermometer inside a mitten. Tie the end shut with a shoestring or a ribbon to keep out chilly drafts. After five minutes, check the temperature again and write it down.

Now, check the temperature of a second thermometer (or let the first one sit at room temperature for twenty minutes). Put the mitten on your hand and slip the thermometer inside against your palm. Check the temperature after five minutes.

The temperature will be higher than on the first test. How much higher is the reading?

You provided all the extra heat.

RIDDLE

Which moves faster, heat or cold?

ANSWER: [illegible]

Gorp and Other Goodies

YOUR BODY'S natural furnace needs fuel to make heat. When you're exploring outside in the cold, your body needs one thousand extra calories per day. To supply this needed energy, whip up a batch of gorp or other high-energy food to munch as you explore.

GORP

Any combination of nuts, sunflower seeds, M&M's, raisins, shredded coconut, butterscotch chips, and whatever else you want to add.

FRUIT BITES

Chop up dried dates and raisins. Mix with peanut butter and flaked coconut. Shape into balls and roll in chopped nuts.

Off the Top

MORE THAN fifty percent of your body heat is radiated away through your head. Covering up your head and neck is "top" priority. A wool sock hat and a scarf make a good combination. Or you can wear a *balaclava*. A balaclava is as heavy as a sock hat but rolls down to cover everything except your eyes and nose.

On the Bottom

YOUR FEET are another area of major heat loss because they conduct heat away to the ground. For the best insulation, start with thin, snug-fitting nylon or wool-blend socks. Wear wool socks over these.

Two pairs of socks will not only keep your feet cozy, but they will also prevent blisters. Blisters develop when your feet rub against your socks. With two pairs of socks, the rubbing is between sock layers.

Rubber boots are good protection against cold, wet weather. But if you plan to hike any distance at all, you'll need winter hiking boots. These have rubber lowers and leather uppers.

THE COLD TRUTH

Exposed skin freezes when the temperature is -34°C. (-29°F.) or lower. A temperature of 10°C. (50°F.) won't bother a weather-dressed person.

If that person is in 10°C. (50°F.) water or completely wet clothes, however, death will occur from loss of body heat within 3 hours.

Weather Myth

The faster a woolly bear caterpillar moves, the sooner cold weather is coming.

Warm Bird

WATCH A BIRD on a cold day. It will fluff up its feathers until it looks like a puffy ball. The feathers hold in the bird's body heat. If you don't think feathers are enough to keep warm, remember that the best cold-weather garments are stuffed with goose or duck feathers. For its weight, down is the warmest stuffing available.

Down-filled clothing does have two disadvantages: 1) it's too warm when you're very active, 2) when it gets wet, down is like wearing a sponge.

Hang onto That Heat

STAYING WARM is a lot easier than trying to warm up when you're cold. What you wear exploring will be your number one protection against heat-stealing wind and water.

Wool is the best material for winter clothing. Wool traps your body heat. It also draws moisture away from your skin to prevent your heat from being conducted away. Wool is a super insulator because it can hold in heat even when it is completely soaked.

Find out how good an insulator other kinds of materials are. You'll need a quart jar, a long-handled spoon, and two-inch squares of wool (one hundred percent wool), cotton, nylon, and polyester.

Fill the jar nearly full of water. Place the wool square on the surface of the water and poke it toward the bottom with the spoon. Watch the air bubbles rush to the surface as the wool is submerged. These air bubbles are trapped air escaping. The more air the material can trap, the better it will hold in your body heat.

Release the wool square. When it floats, poke it under again. Bubbles popping up this time show the ability of wool to continue to trap air even when wet.

Repeat this test with each of the other cloth samples. Compare their ability to trap air to that of the wool square. Which material is second best?

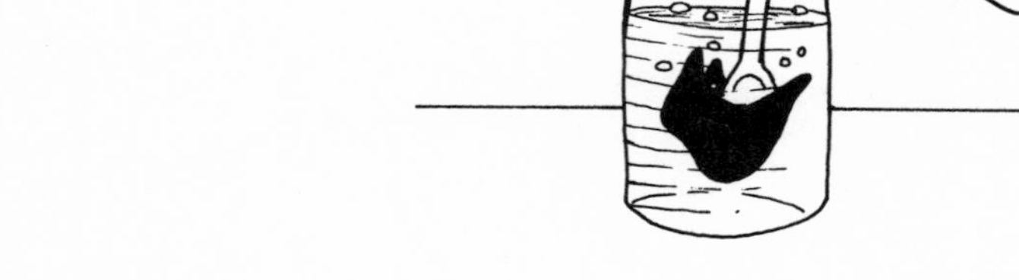

Dressing Warmly

THE SECRET to staying warm and comfortable is layering. Like fluffed up fur or feathers on animals, layers of clothing trap air to prevent heat loss. Layers also allow you more freedom of movement. You can shed outer garments when you're more active and generating extra heat.

Remember, sweating can be like falling into a lake. Heat loss is rapid when your skin becomes wet.

To be really warm when it's cold outside, you should wear:

A hat that covers your ears

A T-shirt (Wool-blend long johns are best. Cotton holds sweat next to your skin.)

A windproof jacket with tightly fitting cuffs

Wool, wool-blend, or corduroy slacks

A scarf to keep cold air from slipping inside your collar

1 or more thin wool sweaters (over or instead of shirts)

Mittens

Wool-blend underpants

2 pair of socks

Boots

Warm Eskimos

WHERE ESKIMOS LIVE, it is often -51°C. (-60°F.) in the winter. Clothing in such a cold climate is a matter of life or death. While many Eskimos today wear down jackets and other manufactured articles of clothing, the traditional items are still appreciated for keeping warm in icy, Arctic winter weather.

Long fox fur jackets with a hood (women with babies have a hooded pouch on the back of their jacket)

Skin stockings

Kamiks (sealskin boots) Men have fox fur trim at the top of theirs to keep out the cold air. A woman's kamiks are long enough to join fox fur underpants.

Dried grass is sandwiched between the kamiks' double soles for insulation.

Birdskin undershirts with feathers turned inside (That must tickle!)

Mittens made of sealskin or caribou skin

Men wear polar bear trousers with the fur out

This is year-round outdoor clothing except in the summer a lightweight seal coat replaces the fox fur coat. Summers in the Arctic are far from balmy.

THE PEOPLE

Eskimo is a Creek Indian word meaning "eaters of raw meat". Eskimos call themselves Inuit *which means "the people".*

A TILUGTUT

This is a small wood or bone sword used to beat snow out of clothing before someone comes inside. Wet clothes would freeze stiff when the person went back outside.

BOO HOO

What's the saddest article of clothing?
Blue jeans.
You'll be sad too if you go out in the cold wearing denim. Jeans offer no insulation, and when wet, denim becomes as cold and stiff as aluminum foil.

THAT'S INCREDIBLE

The bodies of Arctic insects contain a kind of antifreeze. These insects can freeze and thaw out without being hurt. The Arctic beetle can withstand temperatures as low as -34°C. (-30°F.).

Frostnip, Frostbite and Hypothermia

NOT ONLY does it feel uncomfortable to get cold, it can hurt you. Your heart, lungs, brain and other body organs don't work well unless they are about 37°C. (99°F.). As a natural defense, your body will draw heat from other parts (legs, feet, arms, hands, ears, and nose) to keep your body core warm.

Frostnip happens when the skin is deeply chilled. This is a warning stage. Work on warming up as soon as an area feels numb and the skin looks very pale. The fastest way to warm up a frostnipped area is to place it in warm (not hot) water until feeling returns. If this isn't possible, put the frostnipped part against a warm body area.

Frostbite is much more serious. The skin looks white, yellow-white, or blotchy-blue. The area is not just numb. It is frozen. A doctor needs to treat frostbite quickly or permanent damage could be done.

If your core temperature drops below 35°C. (95°F.), you will begin to shiver so hard that you can't stop. Don't wait. Do any of the Sure-Fire Ways to Warm Up listed on page 40. Shivering is a warning signal that you are suffering from hypothermia, too little body heat.

At 32°C. (90°F.), your muscles will begin to cramp. By the time your temperature drops to 30°C. (85°F.), you will have trouble moving and will no longer be able to do anything to help yourself. When your core temperature drops below 27°C. (80°F.), your life will be in danger. So don't ignore the warning signal. When you start to shiver, go to work on warming up.

Snowblindness

(A Pain in the Eye)

THE LIGHT reflected from white snow on a sunny winter day will make you squint and blink. After a while, a lot of blinking will make your eyes feel tired and painfully dry. A cold cloth held over your eyes will ease the pain, but it's even better to protect your eyes and prevent snowblindness. When you go exploring on bright, snowy days, wear sun glasses.

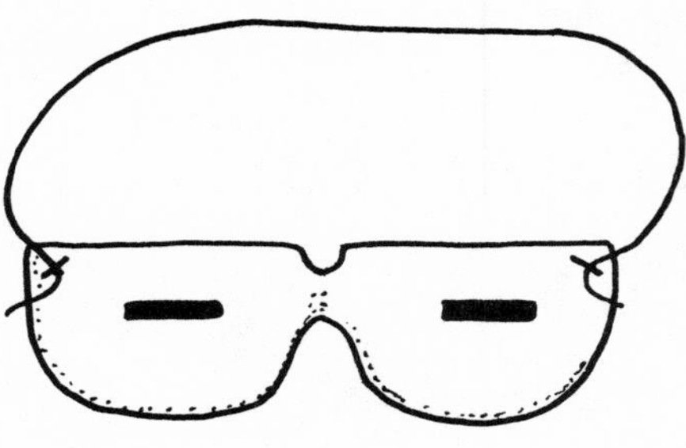

ARCTIC GOGGLES

Where the world is completely covered with ice and snow and there are few clouds to shade the sun, sunglasses aren't enough. Special Arctic glasses wrap around the eyes and have tiny slits to look through.

You can make your own Arctic goggles. Cut a pair from posterboard. Make the goggles big enough to curve around the sides of your face. Cut narrow eye slits, and staple on a piece of elastic to hold the goggles in place while you're exploring.

NEVER

Never rub frostnipped or frost-bitten skin to warm it. Rubbing can tear the injured skin.

Sure-Fire Ways to Warm Up

Drink hot tea (Tibetans do this)
Wear a single bulky wool sweater (raises body temperature 3.7°)
Wear two thin wool sweaters (raises body temperature 5°)
Drink hot cocoa
Huddle next to another warm body
(If you curl up with a big, hairy dog, be sure the dog doesn't have fleas)

Yummy Recipe for Instant Cocoa

(guaranteed to warm your insides and delight your tongue)

1 can Nestlés Quick
1 pound powdered milk
2 cups powdered coffee creamer*
*(optional—makes the cocoa creamier)

Keep this in a jar with a tight lid. When you're ready for a warm taste treat, pour one-fourth cup of this mixture into a cup. Fill the cup with boiling water. Stir and top with miniature marshmallows.

RIDDLE

What good quality does the North Pole remind you of?	ANSWER:

Now that you know how to stay warm,
go outside to try these investigations.

Oddball Water

IN MOST SUBSTANCES, added heat energy makes molecules spread apart. The substance expands. If heat energy is removed, the molecules move together, and the substance contracts.

Water is an oddball. Besides becoming cold and hard, a surprising change takes place in water as it freezes. Follow these directions to see what happens.

Fill a paper cup completely full of water

Put the cup outside if the temperature is below freezing. If it isn't cold enough outside, put the cup in the freezer section of the refrigerator. Check the cup every half hour as the water freezes.

Notice that the water freezes on top first. Why do you think it froze there first? What happened to the water as it froze? (See page 43 for the answers)

RIDDLE

> *What often strikes you in the face, and yet you can never see it?*
>
> ANSWER:

Ice Puzzlers

WATCH AS ICE begins to form in your neighborhood. Is there a pond or a lake near your house? Go looking for puddles. Be an ice detective and look for icicles hanging from the edges of roofs or wherever you can find them.

What's the longest icicle you can find? Where is it hanging? Why do you think it formed there?

Why do icicles form on the edge of a roof? (See page 45)

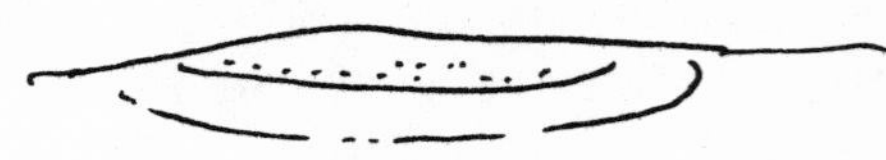

If you find frozen puddles, jump on them. They will crack and collapse with a wonderful crunch. Frozen puddles are usually hollow. Why? Where did the rest of the water go? (see page 45)

A pond or lake will freeze first around the edges in the winter and melt first along the edges in the spring. Why does the water freeze and melt there first? (See page 45)

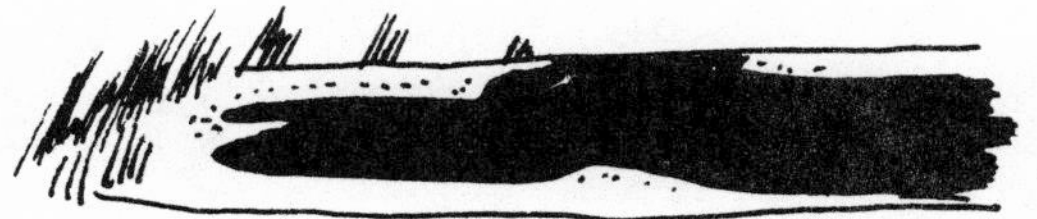

ODDBALL WATER ANSWERS

Water freezes on top because the surface radiates away its heat energy first. The heat escapes into the air.

As water freezes, it expands. The ice pokes up above the top of the cup.

Icicles

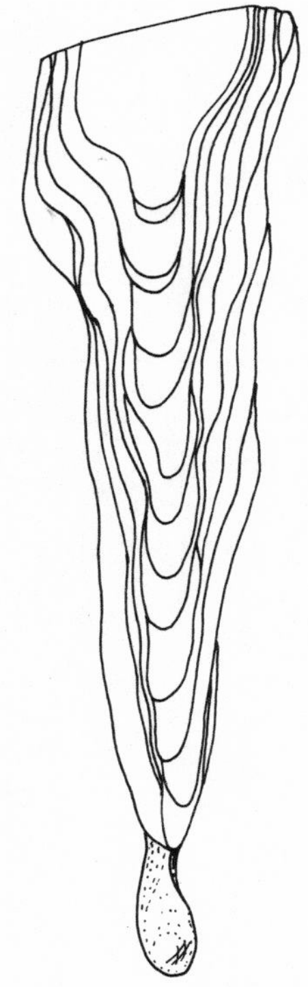

THE PICTURE on the left shows how an icicle would look sliced open. Icicles can be found hanging from tree limbs, rock ledges, roof edges—wherever water drips from an overhang while the air temperature is cold enough to freeze it. Icicles can grow to be several meters (about six feet) long.

The tip of an active and still growing icicle is a drop of water. Water also forms a track from the feed source down the side of the icicle. Eventually, this track freezes over forming a vertical rib, and water streaks down a new path. A horizontal ring forms around the icicle each time it grows longer. You may also be able to see bubbles of trapped air in the icicle.

How Much Weight Can a Frozen Lake Hold?

THESE FACTS are only for clear lake ice. River ice has undercurrents and is less safe. For heavily traveled ice and early winter conditions, the thickness should be doubled.

ICE THICKNESS IN CENTIMETERS *(Inches)*	MAXIMUM LOAD
5 (2)	*One person walking*
7.5 (3)	*Group walking single file*
18.75 (7.5)	*Car or snowmobile*
20 (8)	*Light truck (2½ tons)*
25 (10)	*Medium truck (3½ tons)*
30 (12)	*Heavy truck (8 tons)*

If you aren't sure how thick the ice is, assume it's too thin to walk on.

ICE PUZZLERS ANSWERS

ICICLES:	*The sun's warmth or heat radiating through the roof melts the snow. If the air is still below freezing, the running water refreezes as it drips over the edge of the roof.*
PUDDLES:	*After a puddle freezes over, some of the remaining water sinks into the ground.*
LAKE:	*The dirt or rocks along the edge of the lake lose heat more quickly than the water in the winter and absorb heat more quickly in the spring. This effects the water closest to the shore. Also the shallow water doesn't circulate as much as the deeper water. This speeds the freezing and melting of the surface water.*

Cool Challenge

WHEN THE WEATHER gets above freezing, ice starts to melt. But not all the ice melts at the same time. Think about the places where ice lingers around your neighborhood. Are they sheltered from the wind? Do the sun's warming rays reach that spot for only a short time each day?

Before refrigerators, people used ice boxes to keep their food cool. Large blocks of ice were put inside the box and replaced when they melted. In northern parts of the United States, winter was the time to cut blocks of ice from frozen lakes. These blocks were stacked in barns and coated with layers of sawdust. Sometimes whole towns worked together on this project and shared the stored ice. Every effort was made to store the ice so that the summer's heat wouldn't reach it. If the summer wasn't too hot, ice blocks would still be available for ice boxes as late as the Fourth of July.

How long can you keep ice from melting? Collect fifteen ice cubes (they should all be about the same size). Choose three locations close to home to stash your cubes. Leave a pile of five cubes in each spot. Check your piles of cubes every day. As the weather gets above freezing, the race is on.

How well did you do? Were the cubes at any of your locations one of the last icy spots to melt? The next time the weather turns cold where might be a better place to stash some ice?

RIDDLE

What stays hot no matter how cold it gets?

ANSWER:

WHAT CAUSES WINTER STORMS?

You can find out and make your own weather forecasting instruments to predict them. Winter storms, snow, and some very special holidays are strictly seasonal. And that's what the next chapter is all about.

3. STRICTLY SEASONAL

Weather Wary

SEVERAL YEARS AGO, two University of Colorado students headed into the Rockies during the Thanksgiving vacation. They planned to spend several days hiking and camping out. Since the weather was unusually warm and dry, they didn't bother to pack any heavy winter clothes. They also didn't bother to check an extended weather forecast.

During their second night out, a blizzard hit. Snow swept over the mountains, and the wind-chill temperature dropped to -62°C. (-80°F.). The students were stranded and in danger of freezing to death.

Luckily, a rescue team found the two in time. Other weather-foolish explorers have been less fortunate.

So before you leave home to explore, even if you're not going any farther than your own neighborhood, you'll want to learn how to build an emergency winter shelter. It also helps to understand what weather conditions create winter storms and to check weather forecasts regularly.

VHF (Very High Frequency) weather stations report every four to six minutes twenty-four hours a day. Forecasts are updated every two hours. A special receiver is needed to pick up these broadcasts, but you can purchase a battery-operated model fairly cheaply.

For a list of VHF weather stations write to:

NOAA (National Oceanic and Atmospheric Administration)
National Weather Service
8060 Thirteenth Street
Silver Springs, Maryland 20910
Attention: W112

Taking Shelter

WHEN YOU GO exploring away from where you can reach a house or a building quickly, carry these emergency shelter supplies:

> 45 meters (50 yards) of nylon twine
> a pocket knife
> a 270 centimeters (108 inches) by 360 centimeters (144 inches) plastic tarp

Then if you can't find a cave or a dense thicket of pine trees to sheild you from wind and driving snow, sleet or rain, you can build your own shelter. A teepee-style shelter is the fastest to put together.

Find three branches about 180 centimeters (72 inches) long. Use the nylon twine to bind the poles together near the top. Then position the poles like a teepee and drape the plastic tarp over them. Be sure the wind is not blowing into the open side of the shelter. And secure the bottom of the tarp with rocks or branches. If possible, make a mat of branches or extra clothing to insulate you from the cold ground.

If you have more time to build a shelter before the storm strikes or if the shelter will have to protect you for longer than an hour, a lean-to is better. Start by tying two sets of poles together to support a ridgepole or tie the ridgepole to two trees. Attach two sloping sidepoles to the ridgepole. If it's snowing, add crossbars between the two sidepoles. The weight of heavy snow can cave in your lean-to.

Drape the tarp over this framework and weigh down the bottom edge to keep out cold drafts. Check to be sure the wind isn't blowing into the open side of the lean-to.

In the city, a lean-to can be built by laying a ridgepole (such as a broom handle) across two garbage cans or by tying it to two posts. Even without sidepoles, the tarp can be stretched over the pole and anchored at the bottom. This makes a quick shelter from a sudden cold rain or icy blasts of winter wind.

RIDDLE

Why can't it snow for two days continually?

ANSWER:

Taking Shelter in a Snow House

AN ESKIMO HOUSE is called an igloo. Even though today most Eskimos live in wooden houses year round, many fathers will teach their sons the art of building a winter igloo from big snow blocks. Eskimos enjoy hunting, and when caught by a winter storm or when the hunting party will stay in the same location for several days, a snow igloo makes a good shelter.

LAMP *(This is a stone bowl filled with oil from seal fat. The wick is made of twisted moss. The lamp is used for heat, light, and cooking.)*
TUNNEL *(Shelters the entrance from the wind.)*
STORAGE AREA *(Used to store meat and fish)*
SNOW BENCH *(The sleeping area is covered with dry heather and seal skins.)*

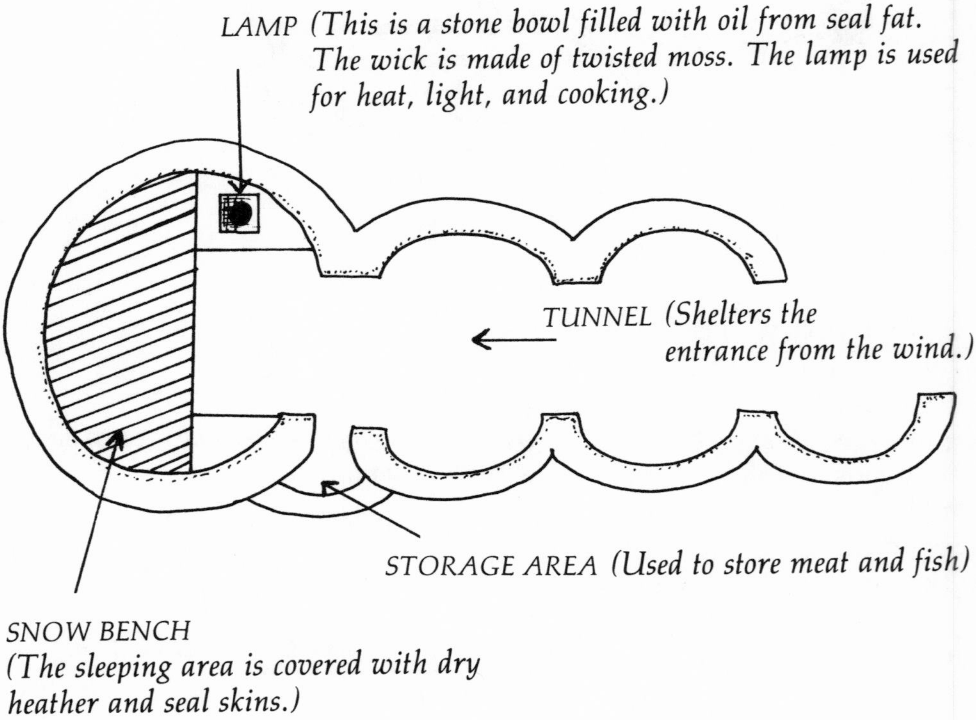

The temperature may be as much as 40° higher inside the igloo than it is outside.

To make a snow igloo, an Eskimo man first cuts big blocks about 37.5 by 72.5 centimeters (15 by 25 inches) and 10 centimeters (4 inches) thick with his knife. The blocks are set up in a circle about 3 to 3.6 meters (10 to 12 feet) across. This outlines the shape of the house.

Two of the blocks are shaved down at an angle. Then the outer rows of blocks spiral up over this foundation. The blocks are placed at a slight incline so that they help hold each other up. Loose snow is packed between the blocks to further support them.

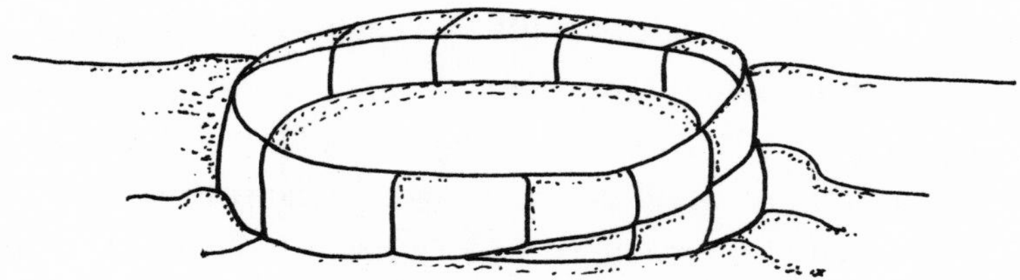

Pretty soon the domed roof takes shape. When there is only a small hole left at the top, a chunk of snow is cut to fit that spot. An even smaller hole is then cut in the top for ventilation. A doorway just big enough to crawl through is dug beneath the block wall so that someone coming into the igloo must climb up to the floor.

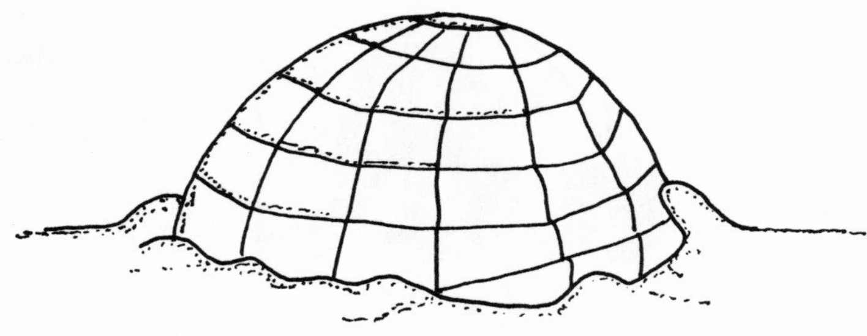

If the igloo is going to be home for some time, a tunnel is added. Sometimes a window is cut out and fitted with a block of clear ice.

Your Own Snow Hut

IT TAKES a lot of practice to build a good igloo, but if there is a lot of snow on the ground, you can build a snow shelter. First, heap up enough snow to make a large mound. Be sure to pack the snow down tightly and then burrow into the pile little by little.

Keep scooping out snow until you have only a thin shell left. Poke a small hole in the dome roof to let in fresh air. Pour water on the outside to seal your shelter with ice.

Cover the floor with branches or a plastic tarp and prop branches against the opening or hang down another piece of plastic for a door. Your body heat will help raise the air temperature inside your hut if you can keep the wind out.

The Making of a Winter Storm

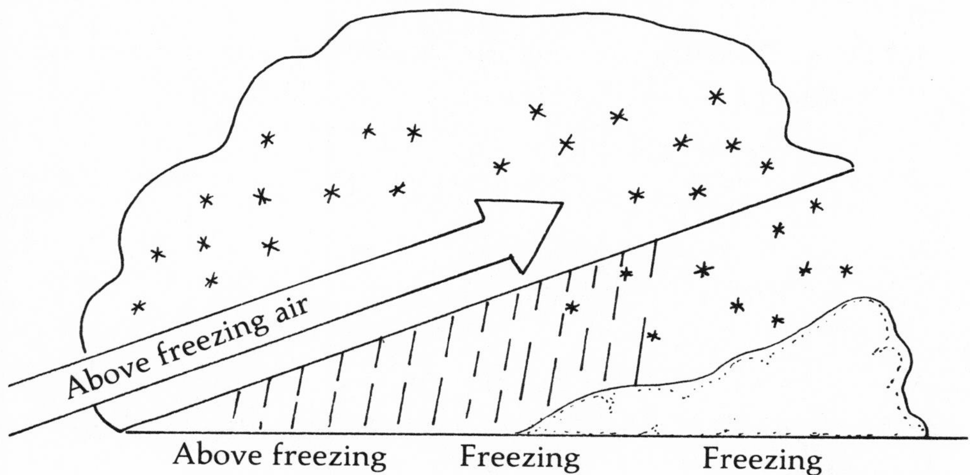

Water evaporates and rises into the upper atmosphere. When this moist air cools, water droplets collect on particles of dust and clouds form.

In the winter, most clouds are 0°C. (32°F.) or colder. Instead of water vapor changing to water droplets in these supercooled clouds, water molecules begin to attach to tiny particles of ice or dust, forming crystals. These crystals are snowflakes.

When there is a lot of water vapor, the crystals grow in size until they are too heavy to be tossed around by the winds circulating in the clouds. The snowflakes tumble toward the Earth.

If the air in the lower atmosphere is above freezing, the snowflakes melt and become raindrops. If the air close to the ground is 0°C. (32°F.) or below, some of these melted flakes may refreeze and fall as ice. Where the lower atmosphere is close to freezing, snowflakes may be mixed with the ice and rain.

A snowstorm occurs only when the air remains at the freezing point all the way from the clouds to the ground.

Predicting a Winter Storm

WINTER STORMS occur when the amount of moisture in the air (relative humidity) is high and there is a storm front (low pressure area) present.

These simple weather instruments will help you forecast winter storms.

HYGROMETER

A hygrometer is used to measure the amount of moisture in the air. The amount of moisture in the air compared to the amount the air could hold is called the relative humidity.

Supplies: a quart or half gallon milk carton, 2 thermometers, 2 rubber bands, scissors, a cotton shoestring, and a metal jar lid.

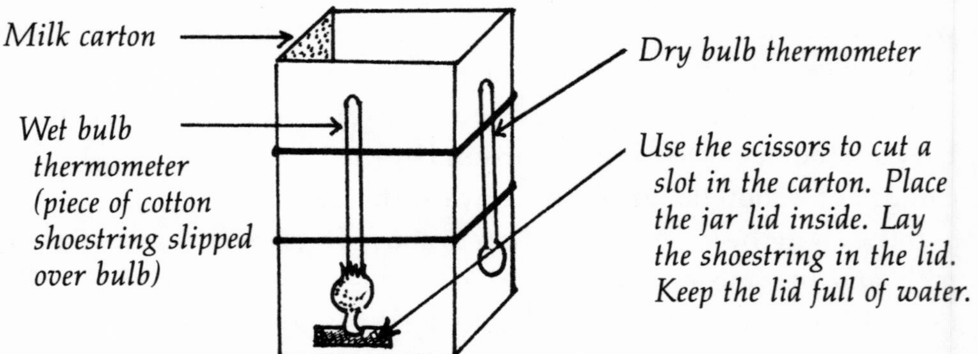
Milk carton
Wet bulb thermometer (piece of cotton shoestring slipped over bulb)
Dry bulb thermometer
Use the scissors to cut a slot in the carton. Place the jar lid inside. Lay the shoestring in the lid. Keep the lid full of water.

Read both thermometers. Subtract the wet bulb reading from the dry bulb reading. Use the chart to find the relative humidity. Remember, in forecasting snow, the dry bulb reading must be at 0°C. (32°F.) or below.

Dry Bulb Temperature in °C/°F

Difference Between Dry-Bulb and Wet-Bulb Temperature

	5/41	6/43	7/45	8/46	9/48	10/50	11/52	12/54	13/55	14/57	15/59	16/61	17/62	18/64	19/66	20/68	21/70	22/72	23/73	24/75
1	86	86	87	87	88	88	89	89	90	90	90	90	90	91	91	91	92	92	92	92
2	72	73	74	75	76	77	78	78	79	79	80	81	81	82	82	83	83	83	84	84
3	58	60	62	63	64	66	67	68	69	70	71	71	72	73	74	74	75	76	76	77
4	45	48	50	51	53	55	56	58	59	60	61	63	64	65	65	66	67	68	69	69
5	33	35	38	40	42	44	46	48	50	51	53	54	55	57	58	59	60	61	62	62
6	20	24	26	29	32	34	36	39	41	42	44	46	47	49	50	51	53	54	55	56
7	7	11	15	19	22	24	27	29	32	34	36	38	40	41	43	44	46	47	48	49
8				8	12	15	18	21	23	26	27	30	32	34	36	37	39	40	42	43
9						6	9	12	15	18	20	23	25	27	29	31	32	34	36	37
10									7	10	13	15	18	20	22	24	26	28	30	31
11											6	8	11	14	16	18	20	22	24	26
12														7	10	12	14	17	19	20

Barometer

A BAROMETER measures air pressure. To make one, you'll need: a thermos bottle, a large rubber balloon, scissors, white glue, a plastic straw, a rubber band, a cereal box, white paper, a marking pen, and a ruler.

Assemble the bottle and the box as shown in the picture. Then place the bottle next to the box so that the straw points to five.

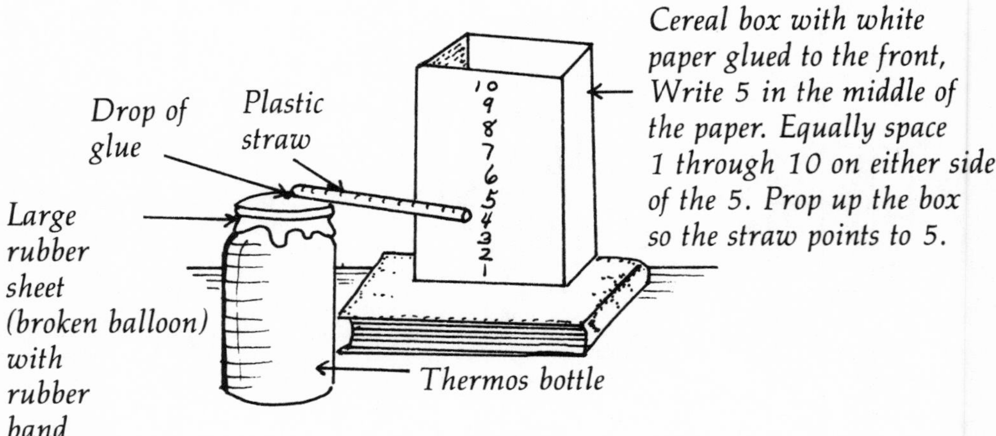
Cereal box with white paper glued to the front, Write 5 in the middle of the paper. Equally space 1 through 10 on either side of the 5. Prop up the box so the straw points to 5.
10 9 8 7 6 5 4 3 2 1
Drop of glue
Plastic straw
Large rubber sheet (broken balloon) with rubber band
Thermos bottle

You can predict a change in the weather by the position of the pointer. When the straw moves to a number above five, air pressure is high (more molecules are pushing down on the balloon). High pressure means fair weather. When the straw points to a number below five, air pressure is low (fewer molecules are pushing down on the balloon). The lower the straw points, the more chance there is for a winter storm.

The reason a thermos is used instead of a jar is for insulation. Heating and cooling of the air trapped inside could change the position of the balloon and effect the reading. The thermos helps prevent temperature changes inside your barometer.

RIDDLE

What do Eskimos get under their eyes when they can't sleep?

ANSWERS:

Let It Snow! Let It Snow! Let It Snow!

SNOWFLAKES are floating down, swirling and dancing in the wind. Snowflakes land on your eyelashes. Wet and feathery—they touch your cheek. Stick out your tongue and catch an icy nibble.

You saw what happened when water molecules froze slowly and became ice. The crazy molecules moved apart—expanded. Well, here's another miracle. Snow.

Snowflakes form when water vapor (water as a gas) freezes so quickly that the vapor becomes a solid without ever changing to a liquid. Each crystal of water needs something to start growing around. This is usually a tiny particle of dust or ice.

Down tumble the tiny flakes until the wind catches them and tosses them up again. Snowflakes stick together, grow bigger, and plunge back toward earth.

Up and down, the crystals rise and fall until they are too heavy for the wind to sweep back into the clouds. Then they drift toward the ground. Occasionally, snowflakes grow as big as the palm of your hand before they start their final descent.

If you hurry outside while the snow is falling, you'll be able to take a close look at the frozen crystals. You may even want to permanently preserve a few.

Snowflake Bentley

SOME OF THE PEOPLE in Jericho, Vermont, thought Wilson Bentley was crazy. A lot of people thought he was strange, loving winter the way he did. Bentley could be found outside even during a blizzard, running around trying to catch snowflakes or trying to photograph them. But finally on January 15, 1885, his efforts paid off. Wilson Bentley became the first person to successfully take a picture of a snow crystal through a microscope.

Bentley took over six thousand photographs of snowflakes during his lifetime and proved that no two crystals are ever the same. He made snowflakes popular. His photographs were copied for everything from wallpaper to jewelry. He became world-famous, but he didn't try to get rich from his work. Wilson Bentley was happy just sharing the beauty of snowflakes with others.

Catching Your Own

WHILE NO TWO snowflakes are ever exactly alike, they are all hexagons (six-sided crystals). Snowflakes take several main shapes.

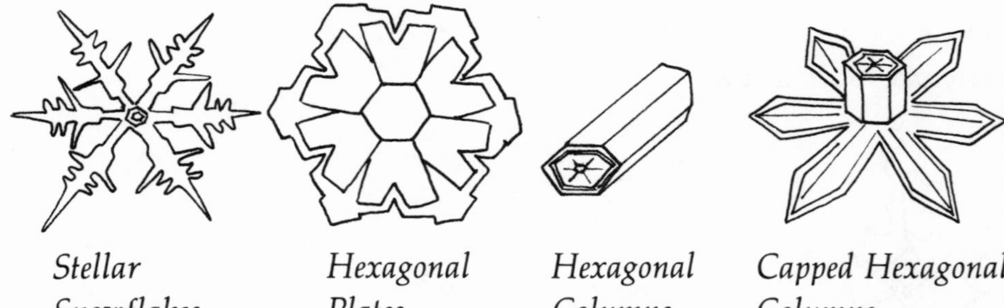

Stellar Snowflakes — *Hexagonal Plates* — *Hexagonal Columns* — *Capped Hexagonal Columns*

If you want to catch some snowflakes, chill a clean glass slide or a small mirror in the refrigerator. Take the cold glass outside and allow a few flakes to collect on it. You may need a magnifying glass to see the snowflakes if they are very small.

When the snowflakes are as big as your palm, don't try to catch them.

DUCK!

To preserve snowflakes so you can even take them inside with you, you'll need a can of plastic spray—the kind artists use on chalk drawings. (Krylon Spray Coating number 1306A works well.) Chill the spray along with the clean glass slides. Carry the slides outside on a piece of cardboard. This keeps your body heat from warming the glass.

Spray the slides lightly with the plastic coating. Then allow snowflakes to collect on the glass. Take the preserved snowflakes inside and let the plastic coating completely dry (about fifteen minutes).

Now, you can examine the snowflakes with a magnifying glass or a microscope if you have one. No need to rush. These snowflakes will stay crystal-clear forever.

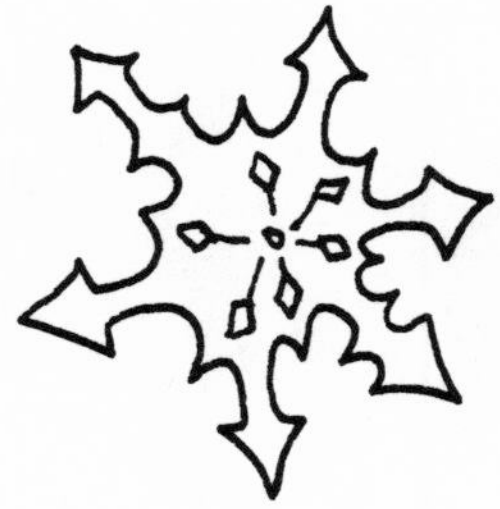

TERRIBLE BLIZZARD

One of the most famous blizzards on record occurred in the winter of 1888. Seventy-five to one hundred centimeters (30 to 40 inches) of snow and ice was dumped on the northeast United States. Without snowplows, entire cities were helpless for weeks. Before the blizzard was over, 400 people had died.

The Winter of the Blue Snow

HAVE YOU EVER heard of Paul Bunyan? He was a giant of a man—and I mean a *real* giant—who ran a lumber camp in the north woods. Paul and his crew of lumberjacks had a lot of adventures, but their chilliest experience was undoubtedly the winter of the blue snow.

Nobody knew why the snow was blue that winter. Maybe it was because the weather was so terribly cold. How cold was it?

It was too cold for thermometers to measure. The men each had sixteen blankets to sleep under, but they still couldn't keep warm. Shot Gunderson, the head sawyer, slept under forty-two blankets one extra cold night. He got lost trying to find his way out from under that huge pile, and it took him three whole days to uncover himself. Poor fellow nearly starved to death before he made it to the cook shack.

Not that eating was easy once you got to the table. When Hot Biscuit Slim, the cook, set coffee out to cool, the steaming brew froze so fast that the ice was hot. The men had to eat with their mittens on because the hot biscuits froze solid before they went the distance from plate to mouth.

Conversations around the bunkhouse were slowed down mightily that super-cold winter. Words froze as fast as they were spoken. Piles of icy words had to be heaped behind the stove because nobody could tell what had been said until the words thawed out.

About the time summer was due, the weather got cold again, and the blue snow kept right on falling. Snow drifts piled up sixty meters (200 feet) deep in places. Elevators were built to carry the men from their bunkhouses to the surface. To reach the forest, Paul had to scoop out holes and lower his men down to the trees. Once cut, the logs had to be hauled out with long ropes.

What? You don't believe a word of this story? It's the absolute truth. Why even today the lakes and rivers are bright blue from the melted blue snow. That's why the far north country is called, "the land of sky-blue water."

How Heavy Is Snow?

ONE FLAKE doesn't weigh very much, but an average 25 centimeter (10 inch) snowfall covering an acre of land weighs 4,972,000 kilograms (226,000 pounds).

Let's say 37.5 centimeters (15 inches) of snow has fallen, and you have to shovel a sidewalk that is 15 meters (50 feet) long and 1.5 meters (5 feet) wide. Without even counting the weight of the shovel, this job will mean lifting 877.5 kilograms (1,950 pounds) of snow.

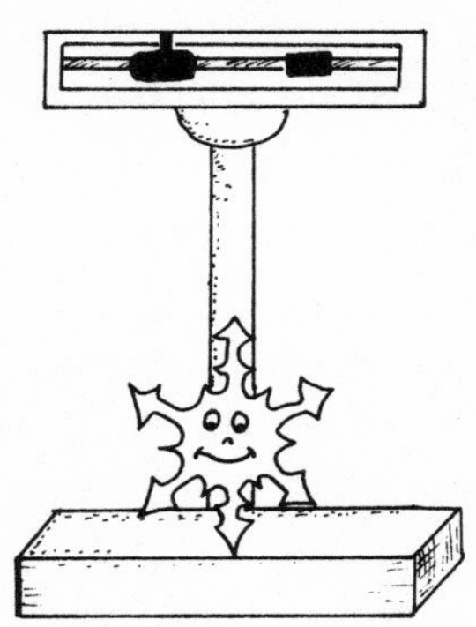

Maybe shovels should be labeled: "Be careful! Shoveling snow can be dangerous to your health."

Measuring Snow

THE FLUFFY white flakes are all over everything. Ridges of snow edge the tree limbs. Your bicycle seat has a snow cushion. So how much snow fell at your house?

There's a snow drift against the side of the garage but only a thin coating of snow on the driveway. Each direction you look, there seems to be a different amount of snow piled on the ground.

Just sticking a meterstick into the snow won't give you a true measurement. As you've already discovered, the wind does a lot of snow moving and sculpturing. The best way for you to measure snowfall is to make a snow guage.

All you need is a can with a wide mouth and straight sides. Attach a strip of tape to one side of the can and use a ruler to mark centimeters and millimeters on the tape.

Place the can outside in an unprotected area. When the snow stops falling, check the can. The number of centimeters inside will be approximately the number of centimeters that fell.

If the wind has done a lot of snow-sculpturing, you may want to go hunting for the deepest drift. Unless the snow is really heaped up, a meterstick will be enough. Poke the stick straight down into the deepest part of the drift. To search for even deeper drifts, mark centimeters on a broom handle.

Good hunting!

PUZZLER

Why do drifts sometimes have an overhanging curl? (See page 66).

Wind Pointers

SNOW DRIFTS can tell you which way the wind was blowing. When the wind strikes one side of an obstacle like this fence, it slows enough to drop its load of snow. Drifts point the direction the wind was heading.

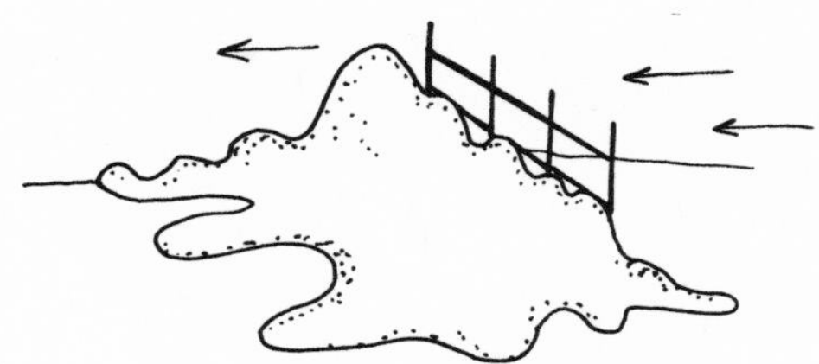

WEATHER TRIVIA

U.S. greatest 24 hour snowfall—190 centimeters (76 inches), April 14-15, 1921 in Silver Lake, Colorado.

WEATHER MYTH

A lot of winter snow means the summer crops will be good.

So Much Snow

ONE-FOURTH of the land in the northern hemisphere is covered by snow in the winter. The snow usually remains in these areas for four months.

How to Make a Snow Angel

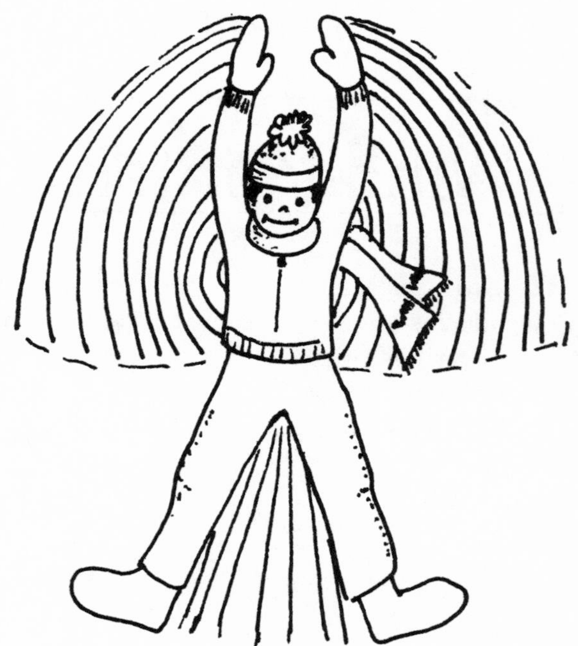

1. Lie down in the snow with your legs together and your arms at your side.

2. Make your arms and legs move as if you were doing jumping jacks.

PUZZLER ANSWER

When wind reaches the edge of a wall, a building roof, etc., it slows down slightly. This causes any snow that the wind was carrying to be dropped and a curl builds up.

Snowball Fight on July Fourth

MAKE SNOWBALLS when the snow packs well. Put the snowballs in plastic bags. Seal the bags and put them in the freezer. On July Fourth, take the snowballs out and let them thaw for a few minutes. Then enjoy a snowball fight in the hot sunshine.

Wet Stuff

SOMETIMES THE SNOW is dry and fluffy. Othertimes it is wet and sticks together easily. It's the wet stuff that makes good snowballs and snow sculptures. But how wet is the snow outside right now?

After the snow has stopped falling, fill your snow gauge with 25 centimeters (10 inches) of snow. Let the snow melt.

In an average snowfall, 25 centimeters (10 inches) of snow will melt down to 2.5 centimeters (1 inch) of water. How much drier or wetter than average was this snowfall? You might want to keep a record of each snowfall this winter to compare the amount of moisture in each. During which months are the snowfalls the wettest?

COLORFUL SNOW

Snowflakes are really clear. The way they reflect light makes them look white.

Snow looks blue or purple in shadows. Snow may turn black when dirt settles on it.

Tiny plants called algae can grow in snow. When this happens, the algae may make the snow look pink, red, yellow, green or blue.

Dirty Snow?

AFTER YOU'VE MELTED 25 centimeters (10 inches) of snow to check for water content, test for visible pollutants. Cover a glass with a clean white paper towel. Then pour the snow-water into the glass through the towel.

How clean is the towel after the water passed through it? Rub your fingers across the paper. Do you feel any particles of dirt? For a real shocker, repeat this test after the snow has been on the ground for several days.

Sometimes snows that have been on the ground for a while begin to look pretty grimy. The next time you're out exploring look for sources of snow pollution.

Watch for these:

cars
factories
trash being burned
overflowing garbage cans
smoke from chimneys
wrappers, cups and bags from fast food restaurants

Are there other sources of snow pollution in your neighborhood? Which seems to be the worst dirt contributor?

RIDDLE

> *What falls often but never gets hurt?*
>
> ANSWER:

Snuggled Under a Snow Blanket

GUESS WHAT—when all those fluffy snowflakes pile up they make a good blanket for the earth.

Don't take my word for it. Find out for yourself.

Put a thermometer outside on top of the snow for thirty minutes. Check the temperature and write it down.

Now, dig a hole in the snow. Lay the thermometer on the bare ground and push the snow back over the hole. After thirty minutes, uncover the thermometer and recheck the temperature.

Surprise! The temperature is slightly higher in the snow than on top of it.

Falling snowflakes trap air between them as they settle. Air, remember, is a poor heat conductor. A blanket of snow acts as an insulator against cold wind. The ground also loses heat more slowly than air or water. So the heat, which continues to escape from the soil all winter, is held in by the layer of snow.

WEATHER MYTH

The wider the light-colored band on a wooly bear caterpillar, the milder the winter.

Plenty of Ice

(How Nice!)

WINTER PROBABLY only lasts a few months where you live. For some parts of the world, winter is the main season.

The areas around the North Pole and the South Pole have the most ice and snow. At the South Pole, there is a continent, Antarctica, that is almost completely covered with glaciers. The only people living at the South Pole are scientists and explorers.

The deep Arctic Ocean is at the North Pole. People live in the cold areas around this frigid sea.

NORTH POLE
Plates of ice cover the Arctic Ocean like a canopy.

TOWN AT THE TOP OF THE WORLD

There is a tiny band of Polar Eskimos living near Melville Bay, Alaska. This nonscientific settlement is farther north than any other community on Earth. These folks live only 1,440 kilometers (900 miles) from the North Pole.

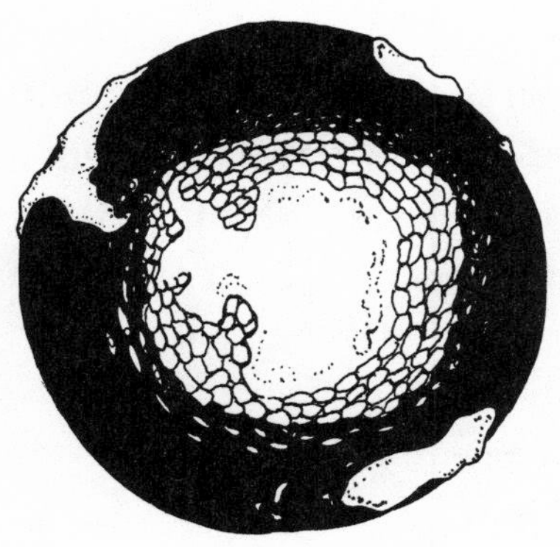

SOUTH POLE
The area of ice in the Antarctic nearly doubles by the end of the winter as plates of ice cover the ocean around it.

GLACIERS

Glaciers form when more snow falls than melts away. The weight of the new snow packs down the old snow. Over many years a giant cake of ice develops.

Today, one-tenth of the Earth's surface is covered by ice. The South Polar Ice Cap in Antarctica and the Greenland Ice Cap are the largest ice-covered areas.

WEATHER TRIVIA

It actually snows less around the North and South Poles than in other parts of the world. In fact, only about 2.5 centimeters (1 inch) of snow falls in a year at each pole. But what comes down is there to stay.

AVALANCHES

In countries where snow falls and builds up on high mountains, the piled-up snow may break loose and crash down. Avalanches move very fast and have great force, crushing everything in their path.

Mountains of Ice

BERG is the German and Dutch word for mountain. Icebergs are mountains of ice that break away from glaciers and float out into the ocean.

While the biggest icebergs form in Antarctica, the greatest number of icebergs can be found floating in the north Atlantic. Greenland produces more than twenty-thousand icebergs each year. Of these ten-thousand to fifteen-thousand may be fairly good-sized bergs.

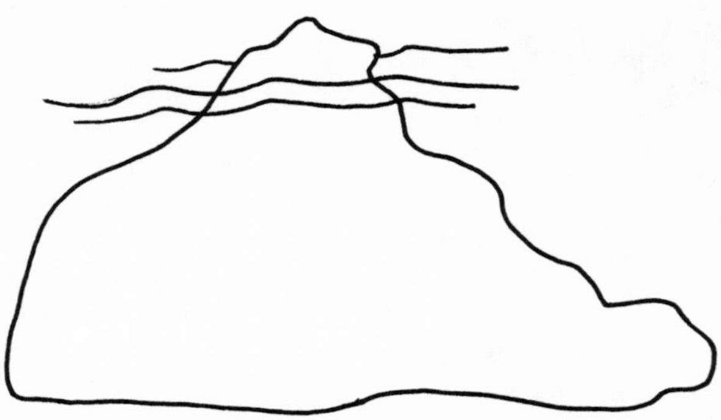

What You See Isn't What You Get

ON APRIL 14, 1912, the giant ocean liner, *Titanic,* set sail from Queenstown, England bound for New York. To reach its destination, the ship had to cross the north Atlantic. Regular watches were kept, but no one was worried. The *Titanic* was considered unsinkable.

Then, unexpectedly, the *Titanic* hit an iceberg. A huge hole was gouged in the ship's hull, and the ocean liner began to sink. The tradedy of this story is that because the *Titanic* was considered unsinkable, not enough life boats were on board and 1,517 people died when the *Titanic* went down.

Why had this accident happened? The sea was calm, and the man on watch had spotted the iceberg. Why couldn't the *Titanic*'s captain avoid hitting the berg?

To solve this mystery, fill a glass nearly full of water. Then float an ice cube in the water. The cube will float the same way icebergs float.

Look at your model iceberg through the side of the glass. You'll see that only about one-third of the cube is above water. By the time the spotter saw the exposed top, the *Titanic* was already dangerously close to the jagged base of the berg.

THE MAIN ICEBERG ROUTE

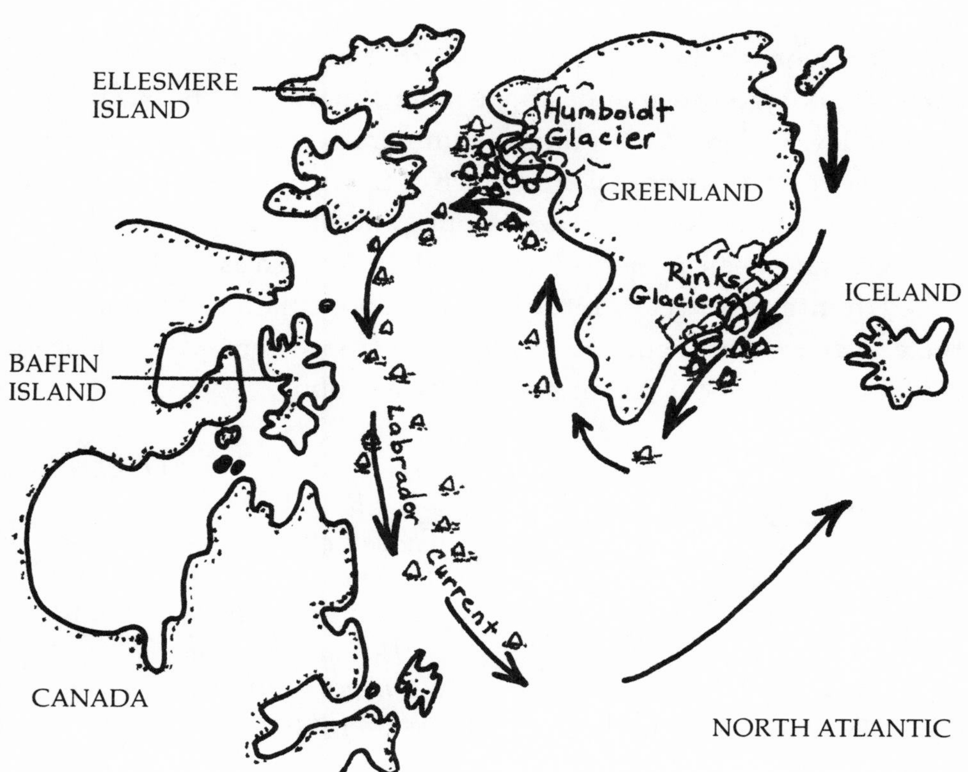

SUPER BERG

The biggest berg ever spotted was 96 kilometers (60 miles) wide and 333 kilometers (208 miles) long. This iceberg covered an area bigger than the state of Vermont.
WHAT A CHUNK OF ICE!

USEFUL BERGS

There has been some talk of towing icebergs to desert areas. Because bergs form from snow, they are fresh water. Big icebergs take from two to ten years to melt. One big berg could yield a lot of fresh water in a thirsty country.

The Big Freeze

PEOPLE who study climates believe that at various times in the earth's history, our planet has tipped more sharply on its axis than it does today. During those times, summers were cold and winters were very cold. Glaciers covered much of Europe and North America as far south as Ohio, Indiana, Missouri, and Illinois.

There have been six periods of glaciation, known as Ice Ages. Each lasted thousands of years. Little is known about plant or animal life in the earlier Ice Ages, but fossils and even frozen remains have been found from the most recent period of glaciation.

THE SABER-TOOTHED TIGER

The saber-toothed tiger lived during the most recent Ice Age. It was a big meat-eater, nearly 90 centimeters (3 feet) tall at the shoulder. It had extra-big upper canine teeth. The saber-toothed tiger is extinct today.

The Woolly Mammoth

(Shaggy Ice Age Beast)

WOOLLY MAMMOTHS looked something like an elephant. But mammoths were slightly smaller, had big curved tusks, a humped back and very tough skin. Oh yes, they also had a whole lot of soft, shaggy fur.

Woolly mammoths roamed across Europe, China, Siberia, and Alaska during the last Ice Age. Their enemies were saber-toothed tigers and people.

Cave men killed these big animals by herding them over cliffs or by digging deep pits to catch them. The people ate the mammoth meat, used the bones for tent frames and as fuel, and made jewelry and musical instruments out of the tusks. The shaggy fur was used for warm blankets and clothes.

In 1901, a mammoth was found frozen in Siberia. Although it was ten-thousand years old, the meat was still fresh. After the beast had been studied, the scientists cooked and ate some of the meat. That's really getting a taste of the past.

Do you think
their noses ran
when it got
really cold?

Something to Celebrate

MOST of our seasonal holidays have ancient origins. Some of the liveliest holidays come when the northern half of the world is cold and dark. This was a relatively free season after a summer of hard work. While the snow fell and the wind blew, there was time to celebrate. Even today, these events entertain, boost spirits, and help people make it through the harsh winter months.

Festival of Light

IN ANCIENT TIMES, the idea of a festival of light was to rekindle the sun's fire. Later ceremonies celebrated the return of a god or goddess from the dark underworld or the rebirth of nature.

The ancient Roman holiday, Saturnalia, lasted seven days and was a joyous event. Everyone was full of hope about the longer days ahead. Gifts were exchanged, and there were open house parties. For at least one day, slaves and masters changed roles.

In Sweden (close to the Arctic circle and very dark at this time of year), the people celebrated the return of longer days. The holiday was called Saint Lucia's Day. A queen was chosen, dressed in white, and given a crown of candles. Maids of honor went with her as she carried her light from house to house. "Star boys," representing the demons and trolls who would be conquered by the revived sun, trailed along behind the procession.

Throughout Europe, a yule log was part of this festival of light. The special log was lit with a piece that had been saved from last year's yule log. Ashes from the log were scattered on fields to help bring good crops during the next planting season.

Hanukkah comes in December and is the Jewish festival of light. This holiday honors an event in Jewish history. Antiochus, the Syrian, had taken over the temple in Jerusalem and forbidden the Jews to worship their God. A group of Jews, the Maccabees, recaptured the temple and rekindled the eternal light which had always burned inside. There was only enough oil for one day, but miraculously, the light burned for eight days.

Christmas

FOR CHRISTIANS, Christ is "the light of the world." No one knows exactly when Christ was really born. Early Christians celebrated this event at various times.

In 350 A.D., Pope Julius I set December 25 as the official birthday of Christ to counteract the pagan festivals of light.

Some Christians disliked the idea of celebrating Christ's birth on a pagan holiday. The Armenians, among others, still celebrate Christmas on January 6.

LUMIÈRES

In some cities, such as Atlanta, Georgia, the custom of "lighting the way for the Christ child" has become part of the Christmas celebration. Plastic milk jugs or paper bags are partly filled with sand, and a candle is placed in the middle of the sand. On Christmas Eve, the lumières are lit, transforming streets and driveways into a twinkling wonderland.

Christmas Star

IN POLAND, the people celebrate the "Festival of the Star" on Christmas Eve. You can make a special Christmas star using wycinaki (pronounced vee-chee-NON-key). This is the Polish art of fancy paper cutting.

Follow these steps to fold the paper. Cut designs into the folded star. The more cuts you make the more delicate and fanciful your star will be.

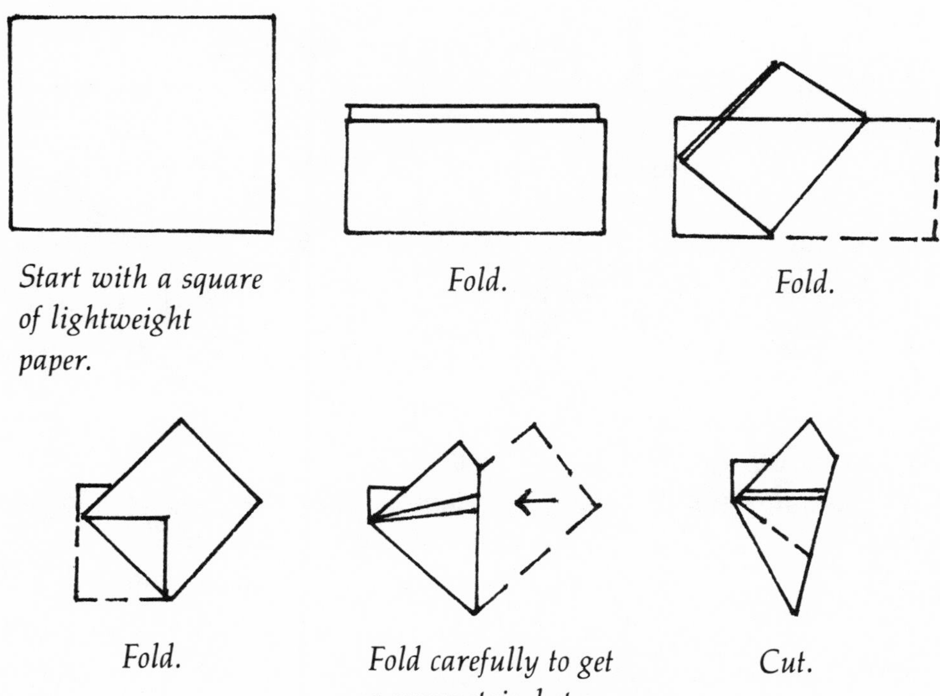

Start with a square of lightweight paper.

Fold.

Fold.

Fold.

Fold carefully to get a symmetrical star.

Cut.

Christmas Is Against the Law

UNDER THE PURITAN GOVERNMENT in England, Christmas was banned as rowdy and pagan. The early colonists in America didn't celebrate Christmas for the same reason. A Massachusettes law enacted in 1659 actually fined anyone who celebrated Christmas.

It wasn't until the nineteeth century when many immigrants were settling in the United States that Christmas customs began to return. One by one, the states made Christmas a legal holiday. Christmas trees became a popular part of this seasonal celebration.

Christmas Trees

SPRUCE
Needles usually 4-sided and attached separately on twigs.

FIR
Flattened, blunt needles attached separately on branches.

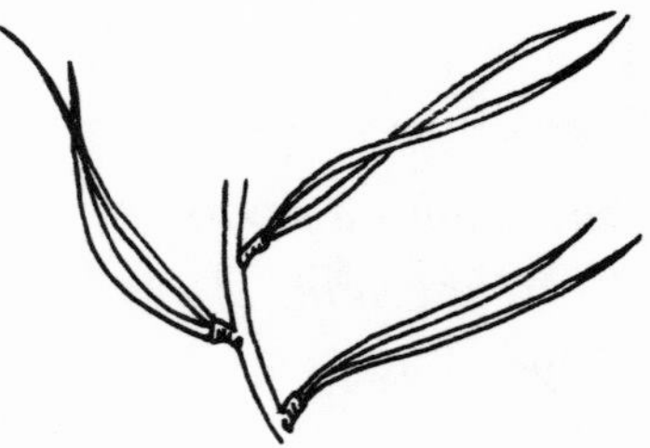

PINE
1-5 needles in bundles with the base of each group enclosed in a papery sheath.

PINING AWAY

You can start your own pine tree. Of course, don't count on using it as a Christmas tree in the near future. Even an average-sized Christmas tree is five to seven years old.

Pick a pine cone from a tree. Choose a cone that is brown and starting to spread open. Place the cone on aluminum foil and put it in the oven on low heat until it is very open.

Shake the cone over a pot of soil. Push the narrow tip of each seed down into the loose dirt. Sprinkle with water. Place the pot in a warm, sunny spot and keep the soil moist. In less than a month, you should have a sprout.

HOG WILD FORECASTS

If a groundhog sees his shadow on February second, there will be six more weeks of winter. If it's cloudy and the furry little rodent doesn't see his shadow, winter is over.

This idea of predicting winter's end is an ancient European myth. Originally, hedgehogs and badgers did the forecasting.

Lacking such critters, German settlers in Pennsylvania started Groundhog Day.

The Punxutawney Groundhog Club in Punxutawney, Pennsylvania has been checking with their local groundhogs since 1898. How often have the Punxutawney groundhogs been right over the years? Not too often.

The Truth About Groundhogs

A GROUNDHOG is also called a woodchuck. Woodchucks stuff themselves on grass and leafy plants until they are almost too fat to move. Then they crawl into their burrow to sleep for the winter.

Several groundhogs may curl up together deep underground. The door to their burrow is sealed with dirt. If water seeps in, they move to a higher room. Sometimes other animals sleep in the spare rooms.

Does a groundhog really wake up on February second? No. The groundhog stops hibernating only when the weather warms up.

DID THE GROUNDHOG SEE HIS SHADOW?

If he did, don't stop exploring yet. There are still plenty of winter days ahead.

4. MAKING TRACKS

Winter Scavenger Hunt

TO START making tracks this winter, go outside for a scavenger hunt. Try to find one item to fit each category. No fair using the same item for more than one category.

Try to find:

Something older than you are.
Something younger than you are.
Something that will burn.
Something that will not burn.
Something that will rot (decay).
Something that will not rot.
A seed.
Something rough.
Something smooth.
Something that will change in the spring.
A bird feather.
A cocoon or an egg case.

RIDDLE

What do you get if you cross a constellation and a toad?

ANSWER:

PUZZLER

Why does a man on snowshoes sink into the snow less than someone without snowshoes?
(See page 87.)

RIDDLE

Why shouldn't you tell jokes while ice skating?

ANSWER:

Winter Moves

EXPLORING in winter can be tough if you try to fight your way across the ice and through the snow. But making tracks doesn't have to be difficult. There are a lot of ways to get around in winter that are fun. Here's a list of some of those ways with their record travel times.

Snowshoes	*1.6 kilometer (1 mile) in 6.23 minutes by Richard LeMay (U.S.) in Manchester, New Hampshire in 1973.*
Speed Skating	*Male: 500 meters (550 yards) at 36.91 minutes by Evgeni Kulikov (USSR) on March 28, 1981. Female: 500 meters (550 yards) at 40.18 minutes by Christa Rothenburger (E. Germany) on March 28, 1981.*
Tobogganing	*Fastest run (sitting position) was 129 kmph (80 mph) in Krynica, Poland.*
Ice Yachting (Sailing on Ice)	*228 kmph (143 mph) by John D. Buckstaff (US) on Lake Winnebago, Wisconsin in 1938 in a 115 kmph (72 mph) wind.*
Snowmobiling	*217.49 kmph (135.93 mph) by Donald J. Pitzen (US) at Union Lake, Michigan on February 27, 1977.*
Dogsledding	*32 kmph (20 mph) No race details available.*

History on Ice

PEOPLE HAVE been trying to slide on ice for almost a thousand years. Since the idea was to glide like a sled, walrus tusks and reindeer bones were strapped onto shoes with leather laces.

But people weren't as heavy as sleds. There wasn't enough friction (rubbing) created to melt the ice under the blade. Without this melting action, sliding wasn't easy. In fact, skaters resorted to using poles (like skiiers do) to push themselves along.

Wooden blades were an improvement, but metal blades were the real answer. Even better was the idea developed in the 1800s of attaching the blades directly to the shoes.

Today, ice skates are specialized. For figure skating, the blades have notches on the toes. These toe picks help grip the ice for leaps and quick stops. Hockey skates have reinforced shoes and blades curved front and back for quick direction changes. Speed skaters have light-weight boots and long, thin blades.

Whatever their special features, the trick to gliding across the ice is still friction. The more the blades dig in, the more the ice is melted. The skates slide through this thin trail of meltwater.

PUZZLER ANSWER

A man on snowshoes sinks in less because his weight is spread out over a larger area. Snowshoes have a bent wood or metal frame 90 centimeters (36 inches) long and about 30 centimeters (12 inches) wide strung with a webbing of leather strips.

RIDDLE

What do you call a frozen policeman?

ANSWER:

COLD HOME

Oymyakon in Siberia is the coldest permanently inhabited town on Earth. On one very cold day in 1964, the temperature in Oymyakon dropped to -71°C. (-96°F.).

Dogs Don't Run Out of Gas

EVEN THOUGH most Eskimos today use snowmobiles, one of the oldest and most dependable forms of Arctic travel is still the dogsled.

The sled (also called a sledge or a *komatik*) is 180 centimeters (72 inches) to 390 centimeters (156 inches) long and about 60 centimeters (24 inches) wide. The back of the sled is built up and has a bar for the driver to grasp. Today, dogsleds are made of wood or metal. Early sleds were made by lashing bones together. The runners on those Eskimo sleds were walrus tusks.

A team of six to twelve Siberian huskies or Alaskan malamutes is used to pull the sled. Eskimos only feed sled dogs every other day because they believe teams run best when the dogs are hungry. To keep their dogs from eating the sealskin harnesses, the drivers file down the dogs' teeth.

Teams are hitched in a gang hitch or a fan hitch. In a gang hitch, the dogs are harnessed in pairs behind a single lead dog. All the lines are attached to a main gang line. In a fan hitch, each dog is harnessed to a separate line which is connected directly to the sled. Fan hitches are used in rough terrain where each dog needs to pick its own course.

With a fan hitch, the whole team isn't lost if one dog falls into a crevasse (deep crack in the ice). Dogsleds average 20.8 kmph (13 mph).

Each winter there is a World Championship Sled Dog Derby in New Hampshire. But the longest dogsled race in the world is held every March in Alaska. The Iditarod (I-dit-uh-rod) Trail Race follows a slightly different course every year but it is always more than sixteen hundred kilometers (one-thousand miles) long and has taken from twelve to thirty-two days to complete. The Iditarod roughly follows the route that gold seekers traveled from Anchorage to Nome in the 1900s.

This yearly race honors the mushers who risked their lives during the winter of 1925. Driving through a blizzard, they carried medicine to Nome in record time, preventing a diptheria epidemic and saving many lives.

Like those brave men, the racers travel day and night, alternately running four hours and resting four hours. Each team stops at only one of the twenty-four check points for a full twenty-four hour rest. People living along the trail kindly take in the weary drivers, offering a meal and a warm place to sleep. Veterinarians at the check points examine each dog and remove any injured members of the team. Racers are allowed to keep going as long as five dogs remain in harness.

Having a strong, healthy team is important to winning. So drivers often tie heavy cloth boots on their dogs' feet to protect them from rough ice. The first twenty teams across the finish line win cash prizes.

Fox and Geese

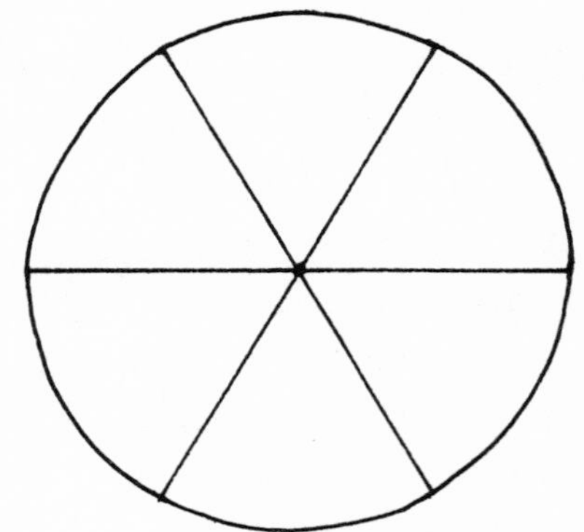

HERE'S a winter game for you and your friends. Tramp a big circle in the snow. Then make six spoke-like paths radiating from a center spot. Play tag, staying just on the paths. The person who is "it" is the fox. Everyone else is a goose. You're safe when you're standing on the center spot.

Into the Winter Frontier

IN THE FAIRY TALE, Hansel and Gretel went into the dark woods dropping a trail of bread crumbs to mark their way back home. It was a good idea, but it didn't work. The birds ate all the bread crumbs, and the brother-sister exploring team got lost.

Going exploring anywhere in the winter is a lot like venturing into the wilderness. Familiar landscapes can be changed completely by a thick coat of snow. A strong wind can cover your tracks and alter landmarks in a very short time.

It's a good idea to know a few basic tricks for finding directions no matter how short your exploring trip might be. North is the direction these methods locate. Once you know where North is, you can figure out which way you need to make tracks.

WHAT TIME IS NORTH?

Be sure your watch is set for the correct time when you leave home. If you're on daylight savings time, add one hour to be on sun time.
To find your direction, point the clock's hour hand at the sun. Divide the distance between this and the twelve spot on the watch. That point on the dial will be aimed South. The opposite point on the watch dial will point North.

Polaris and the Star Gang

WINTER OR SUMMER, if you live in the northern hemisphere, Polaris (also called the North Star) can be counted on to point toward the North Pole. Why?

The Earth's invisible North Pole axis is always aimed straight at this star. The South Pole axis is also always aimed at a certain spot in space. However, there isn't a star to mark that southern point.

People have been watching the stars since the beginning of time. What else was there to do during prime time without television? It

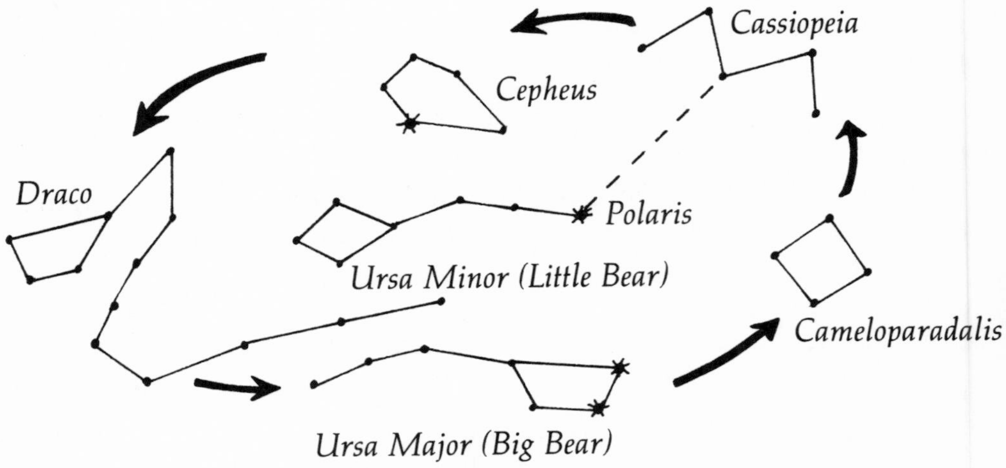

was also easier to see stars without the bright glow of city lights and the blur of polluted air.

To entertain themselves, the star gazers made up stories about star groups called constellations. The favorite sources of stories were the constellations around Polaris. While other constellations were only visible during certain seasons (depending on where the Earth was in its orbit of the sun), the constellations surrounding Polaris were always visible.

These constellations appear to be circling Polaris. In reality, it's the Earth that is doing the turning.

Legend of the Sky Bears

IN THE STORY told by the ancient Greeks, a beautiful woman named Callisto had angered Juno, queen of the gods. As punishment, Callisto was turned into a bear and her son, Arcas, became an orphan.

Years later, Arcas met a bear

while out hunting and was about to shoot it. He didn't know the bear was his mother.

Jupiter, king of the gods, couldn't undo Juno's spell so he turned Arcas into a bear too. Then to reunite mother and son, he changed them into constellations. The star bears have long tails because their tails stretched as Jupiter swung them skyward.

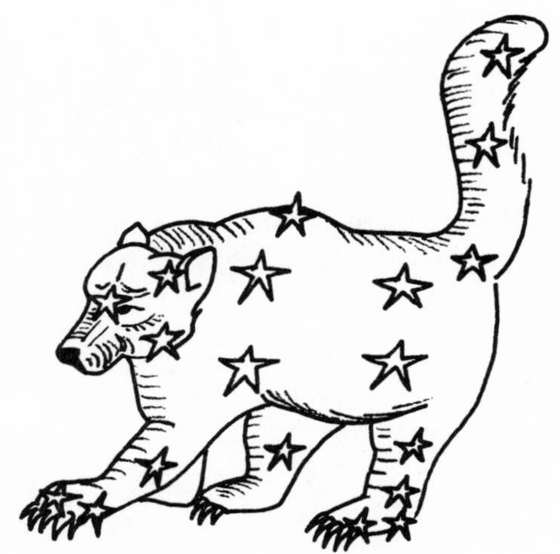

Star Find

TWO TO FOUR people can play.

Divide paper plates into five parts (each player needs a plate). Put Polaris where the lines meet. Label the sections as shown. For a more challenging game, show only the constellation shapes.

Use 3x5 index cards for playing cards. Label five cards for each of the constellations that circle Polaris. Also make two cards for each of these constellations: Orion, Perseus, Taurus, Scorpio, Leo, Canis Major, Aries, Pisces, and Andromeda.

Shuffle the deck. Play by

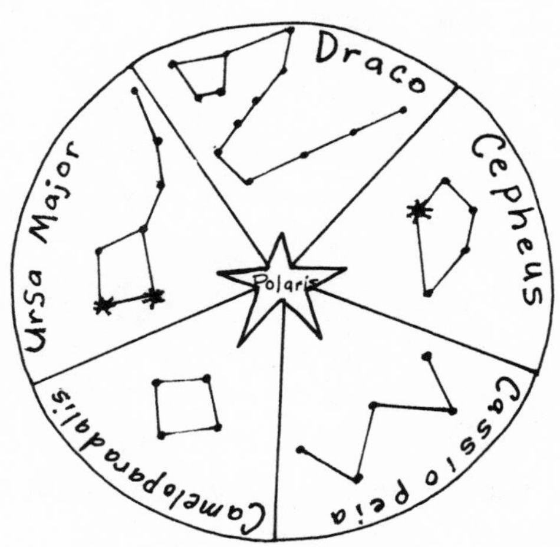

drawing and discarding. If a card is drawn that shows one of the constellations surrounding Polaris, place it on the sky plate. The first player to fill their sky plate is the winner

RIDDLE

Where do Eskimos keep their money?

ANSWER:

STAR SPOTTER

One of the easiest constellations to spot in the winter sky is Orion, the Hunter.

Look toward the South. Find three bright stars in a row. These form Orion's belt. Then locate the rest of the constellation.

Shooting Stars

SHOOTING STARS are really meteors, chunks of nickel, iron, or rock that enter the earth's atmosphere. Friction between the air molecules and this speeding chunk cause it to burn brightly. During its orbit, the earth periodically passes through areas full of these chunks. Then there is a meteor shower.

You can see such a shower during the winter. To spot them, keep your eye on these constellations: Taurus, Leo, Gemini and Boötes. Use books to help you locate these constellations.

A NATURAL LIGHT SHOW

The earth is constantly bombarded with solar energy. But when there is a magnetic storm on the sun's surface, bursts of solar energy strike our atmosphere.

The earth's magnetic force field shields most of the planet, rolling these waves of energy toward the poles. Here the force field is weaker and the energy particles show up as wavering bands of red, orange and green light.

In the North this display is called the Aurora Borealis or northern lights. In the South it is called Aurora Australis. This surge of electricity interferes with radio waves and shorts out power lines.

Early Arctic Explorers

Pythias 325 B.C.	He was a Greek navigator from Marseilles who discovered a distant cold land. He named this place Ultima Thule (Outermost Land). Today it is believed that this was really the coast of Norway.

<table>
<tr><td>Norsemen and
Irish Monks
870 A.D.</td><td>They explored and settled colonies on Greenland and Iceland. These colonies lasted 500 years and then disappeared. Scientists believe that the colonists either died during a period of extremely cold weather or joined the wandering Eskimo bands.</td></tr>
<tr><td>Sir Martin Frobisher
(English) 1576</td><td>Frobisher began the push to explore the far North. Frobisher Bay in the East Canadian Arctic is named for him.</td></tr>
<tr><td>Admiral Cornelius Naij
(Dutch) 1594</td><td>Admiral Naij led the first Dutch polar expedition. It was looking for whales. A town called Smeerenberg (Blubbertown) was built on the northwest tip of Spitsbergen north of Greenland. During the summer months as many as two thousand people lived there to kill the whales for their oil.</td></tr>
<tr><td>William Baffin
(English) 1616</td><td>Baffin discovered Baffin Bay between Canada and Greenland. He also charted three routes to the Arctic Ocean.</td></tr>
<tr><td colspan="2">In 1818, the Royal Geographical Society in London, England offered £20,000 (about $56,000 today) to anyone who could find a northwest passage to the Pacific Ocean. The primary goal of Arctic explorers was to find a passage from Europe to the Orient. But from this point on, exploration of the Arctic became a goal in itself.</td></tr>
</table>

James Ross (English) 1831	On June 1, 1831, Ross located the position of the Magnetic North Pole.

Two Norths

THE REAL NORTH POLE is where the earth's invisible axis points toward the sky. The Magnetic North Pole is near Barthurst Island (off the coast of Canada) about 2,240 kilometers (1,400 miles) south of True North. The compass points to the Magnetic North Pole.

Lost in the Arctic

JOHN FRANKLIN had already spent most of his life exploring the Arctic. He was along in 1831 when James Ross located the Magnetic North Pole.

At the age of fifty-four, Franklin accepted command of what was to be the best equipped Arctic expedition to date. The two ships, *Erebus* and *Terror*, were steamships equipped to push through the pack ice. And the ships carried supplies for three years. Everyone felt sure that this expedition would at last find the northwest passage to the Orient.

On July 26, 1845, the ships stopped at Greenland. Members of the crew wrote home that their next letters would be from Hong Kong. The *Erebus* and the *Terror* were never seen again.

Three rescue expeditions failed to find anymore than Franklin's first winter camp. Finally, in 1854, some Eskimos led searchers to thirty bodies. There was no clue as to where Franklin and the other survivors had gone.

Although the Admiralty called off all rescue attempts, Lady Franklin financed one more. She had a map with directions which had supposedly been given to her by a spirit. Strangely, this map led searchers directly to Franklin's body.

To this day, no one knows why Franklin's expedition failed. As recently as 1932, bodies of men from his crew were found frozen in the ice.

John Franklin failed to find the northwest passage, but through attempts to find him 11,200 kilometers (7,000 miles) of coastline was explored.

The Pole at Last

LIEUTENANT ROBERT EDWIN PEARY of the United States Navy had only one goal. He wanted to be the first person to reach the North Pole.

Unlike other Arctic explorers, Peary took time to learn survival skills from the Eskimos. He used their style of clothing, eating and traveling. His first plan was to reach the North Pole by crossing Greenland. He tried this in 1891 but was stopped when he broke his leg.

The next spring, he set off again. For three years, Peary explored northern Greenland, discovering new territory. But he didn't reach the Pole.

In 1898, Peary wintered on Ellesmere Island. Both of his feet became frostbitten during a long sled journey, and eight toes had to be amputated.

A less determined man would have given up. Peary didn't quit. On April 1, 1902, he set out for the Pole again. This time he got within 288 kilometers (180 miles) before winter storms forced him to retreat.

In 1909, Peary started north one more time. First, an advance group deposited food and equipment so that Peary's team would only have to carry supplies during the last leg of the trip.

On March 1, 1909, Peary and twenty-six men struck out for the Pole with twenty-eight sleds and one hundred and forty sled dogs. With Peary was Matthew Henson, his black aide.

Five days out, open water stopped them. They waited five more days, trying to find a solid route. Some of the Eskimos quit. Finally, ice rafts were cut and the party ferried across the dangerous open water.

Twenty-eight days out, the ice split open while the men were camped. Some of the party was carried away on the drifting ice and had to be rescued. Despite repeated hardships, the men struggled northward.

At last, on April 6, 1909, Robert E. Peary became the first man to reach the North Pole. "The Pole at last," he wrote in his diary. "The prize of three centuries, my dream and goal for twenty years. Mine at last!"

Early Antarctic Explorers

FOR CENTURIES people dreamed of a wonderful land at the South Pole. Since it was so far south, people imagined it as a warm, fertile place—perfect for farming. Not until Captain Cook reported his sightings of great fields of ice did the dream die. But unlike the North Pole, which is an ice sheet floating on the Arctic Ocean, the South Pole is a continent. In fact, Antarctica is a land of fire and ice. Active, smoking volcanoes rise above the glaciers. Antarctica also has an ocean boundary caused by frigid surface water meeting warmer water from the South Pacific and South Atlantic. A thick fog bank forms a wall through which explorers must pass on their way to the strange continent at the bottom of the earth.

Captain James Cook (English) 1770s	*Cook was the first to cross the Antarctic Circle but he never saw the land beyond the pack ice (frozen seawater that floats on the ocean). His reports of whales and fur seals brought many hunters.*
Baron Fabian von Bellingshausen (Russian) 1819–21	*Baron Bellingshausen was the first to sail completely around Antarctica. And he was the first to see the continent.*
James Weddell (Scottish) 1822	*Weddell discovered the Weddell Sea (close to the Falkland Islands and South America).*
James Clark Ross (English) 1840–43	*Ross made the first major exploration of the continent. He discovered Mount Erebus (volcano), McMurdo Sound and the Ross Ice Shelf.*

Ernest Shackleton (English) 1908	*Shackleton discovered new mountain ranges and glaciers. Part of his expedition under Professor Edgworth David found the South Magnetic Pole. He tried to reach the South Pole but failed.*

THAT'S AMAZING

Boiling water thrown into the air when the temperature is below −51°C. (−60°F.) will burst into a cloud of tiny ice crystals.

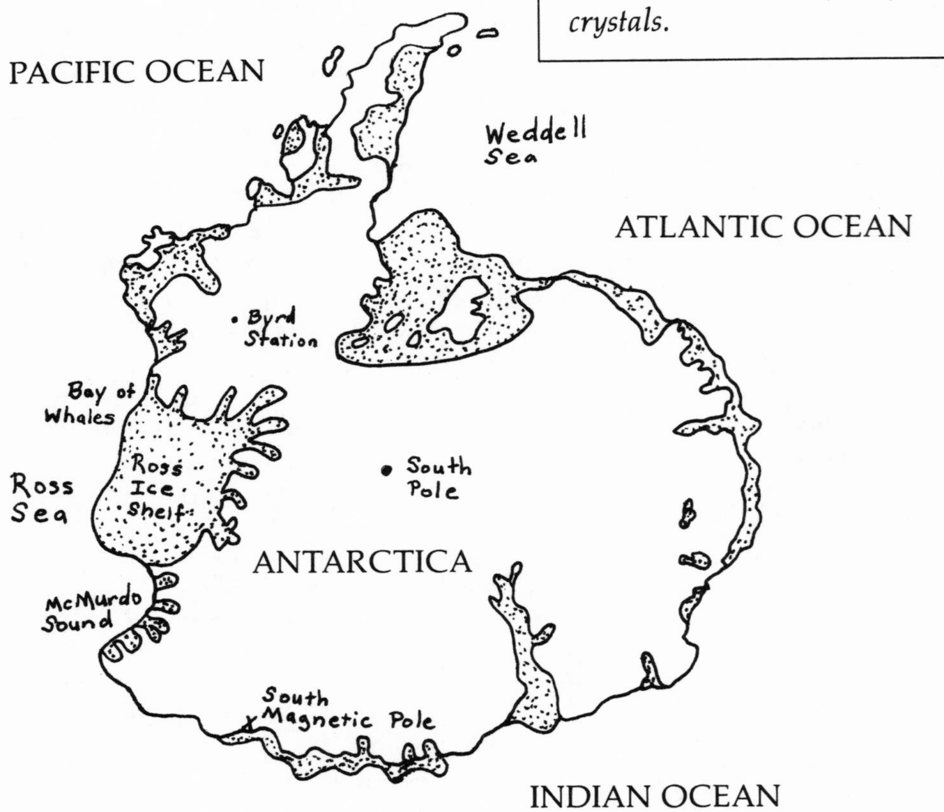

Modern Expeditions

ADMIRAL RICHARD E. BYRD (United States) was the first to fly over the North Pole in 1926. He also led the exploration of Antarctica. To set up his base, Little America, Byrd brought in huts designed to withstand the hostile environment, an electric generator, equipment for bathrooms and a well-stocked library. A French station sits on stilts so snow can blow under the building during blizzards rather than pile up against the walls. And at McMurdo City, the United States Naval Air Station, electricity is supplied by nuclear power. This station has a hospital, a gymnasium, and a bowling alley. The Antarctic Treaty of 1959 set this continent aside as a place where scientists of all nations could work together in peace.

Because the Arctic is only an ice sheet, exploration in the North has been from the air, on the ice and under the ice. The United States nuclear submarine *Nautilus* was the first to reach the North Pole under the ice on August 3, 1958. Repeated trips under the ice have mapped the sea floor and tested the thickness of the ice sheet.

Exploration of the North has been encouraged by the discovery of oil (particularly on the North Slope of Alaska in the Prudhoe Bay Field) and by the importance of this area for defense. Both the United States and Russia have electronic detectors of every kind facing each other across this strategic stretch of ice.

The resources of the North are already being tapped and work goes on to discover resources in the South. Perhaps the greatest offering that the Poles will make to people in the future is room for expansion. As the warmer areas become increasingly more crowded, people can turn to the Poles as new frontiers to be settled.

EMPTY WORLD?

Bare branches rattle in the cold wind. Snow blows across an already snow-covered yard. You might think that all the wildlife has left or is hibernating. The plants look dead. From your window, the world looks empty—deserted.

Take a closer look. Bundle up and go exploring. You'll be surprised how full of life winter really is.

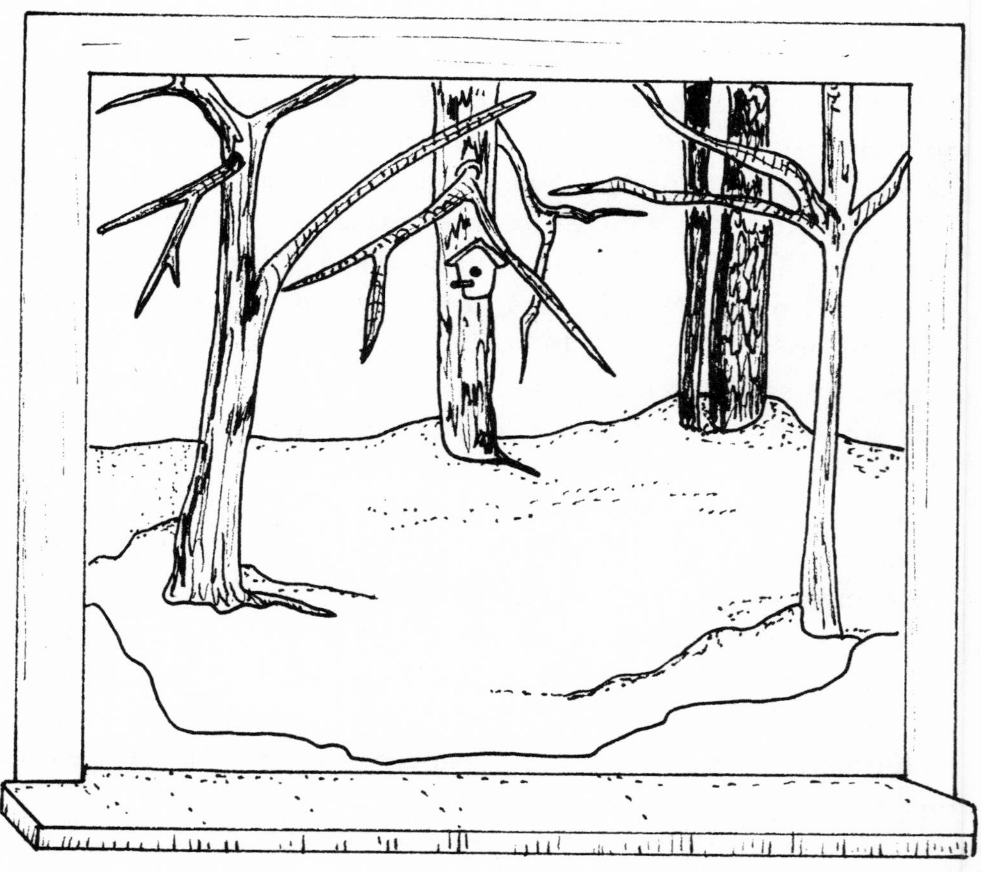

5.
WILD IN WINTER

The Tweet Treat Diner

YOU CAN GET a good look at the birds that spend the winter in your neighborhood if you invite them to dinner. Here are directions for three bird feeders that you can make to coax your feathered guests.

The kinds of birds that come to eat at your feeder will depend on the type of food you serve. Birds such as sparrows, cardinals and juncos eat only seeds. Other birds such as woodpeckers and chicadees are normally insect eaters. These birds prefer peanut butter or suet (chunks of fat available at grocery stores).

Peanut Butter Delight

LOOP A STRING around the top of a pine cone. Smear peanut butter on the cone and roll in birdseed. Then hang this feathered diner's delight where the birds will be able to perch and eat.

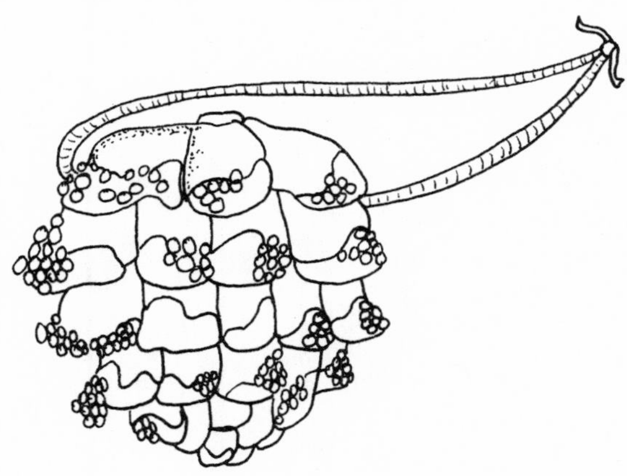

Soft Drink Special

YOU'LL NEED a plastic soft drink bottle, scissors, string, three wire garbage bag ties, and an aluminum pie plate to make this feeder. Follow the directions with the picture to put it together.

Cut off a piece of string 45 to 90 centimeters (18 to 36 inches) long. Poke two holes in the neck of the bottle. Loop the string through the holes and tie.

Cut off the bottom of the bottle. Cut out scallops to allow a flow of seed.

Add seed as needed.

Poke holes in the pan and two opposite sides of the bottle. Attach the bottle to the pan with the ties. Twist the third tie to each of the other two ties on the bottom of the pan.

REMEMBER

Once you begin to feed the birds, they will depend on you to keep the food coming. In bad weather, your diner may be the only meal around. Failure to serve could mean death for some of your regulars.

RIDDLE

Why do Eskimos always have fresh air to breathe?

ANSWER:

Suet a la Mode

BUY ENOUGH suet chunks to fill a cup-and-a-half cup. Melt this fat in a pan over low heat. When the suet becomes liquid, stir in one cup of bread crumbs, one cup of popped corn and one teaspoon of clean sand.

While this fatty mixture cools, cut off the bottom of an empty plastic soft drink bottle. Scoop the partly congealed mixture into this container. If the weather is cold, place the dish outside immediately. Otherwise, refrigerate until the mixture hardens. Then place the dish outside on the ground.

Some birds such as juncos and sparrows prefer to dine on the ground. This makes a good meal for them.

BIRD WATCHING

What kinds of birds come to eat at your feeders? Use bird books to help you identify them. As you watch the birds, think about these questions:

1. What time of day do the birds come to eat? How often do they come?
2. Do the birds come more or less often if the weather stays bad?

TRUE GRIT

The sand was added to the fat mixture because birds need grit to digest their food. Since they don't have teeth, birds swallow pebbles or sand to grind up their food.

3. Do the birds feed one at a time or in groups?
4. Which birds chase other birds away?

Besides the birds, there are a lot of other animals that are active during the winter.

Mice

THESE RODENTS can be found living indoors and outdoors. Field mice spend the winter looking for seeds and berries. Many field mice are caught and eaten by larger winter-active animals.

The snow mouse (also called the collared lemming) lives in the far north. To escape being caught, this mouse grows a white coat. Using a thick pad that develops on their front feet, the snow mice dig tunnels through the snow. After all, it's safer for a mouse—even a white mouse—not to be seen at all. These winter subways may be 18 meters (60 feet) long with many shorter side branches.

Rabbits

THE COMMON cottontail only feels safe leaving its burrow at night. You'll find its tracks but seldom see it.

If you live in Canada, Alaska or the northeast and central United States, you may see a white rabbit in the winter. The snowshoe rabbit grows a white coat and tufts of long hair between its spread-out toes. Padded feet keep it from sinking into the deep snow.

Rabbits will eat almost anything in winter: pine needles, bark and even small birds.

White-Tail Deer

DEER are active all winter. By October, their summer coat of fine, short hair has been replaced with coarse, hollow bristles. This thick coat traps air for added insulation.

Deer live alone most of the year, but in the winter they gather in small groups. It's hard for deer to walk in snow with their small hoofs. So they follow each other and trample pathways. Deer also gather in herds to stay warm. The larger the group the more quickly all available food is eaten. By late winter, there may be nothing for the deer to eat but twigs and small branches.

Red Foxes

RED FOXES hunt all winter. They eat moles, weasels and any small rodents they can catch. Any food left after a meal is buried in the snow for later. Red foxes also dig through the snow looking for apples. They love this crunchy fruit.

Foxes live in dens during the summer while their young are growing up. In the winter, they don't have a permanent home and sleep wherever they can find shelter from wind and snow.

Beavers

BEAVERS build a lodge to protect themselves from winter. This house is made of sticks and plenty of mud. The lodge is built in the water with its floor above water and one or two tunnels leading to underwater exits. The very top of the lodge has only a thin mud covering to allow some ventilation.

In the winter, the beaver family's combined body heat rises as steam from the lodge peak. The beavers seldom go out on the snow or ice because their feet and scale-covered tail freeze easily. Their food supply of bark-covered branches is stored underwater. Aspen bark is their favorite food.

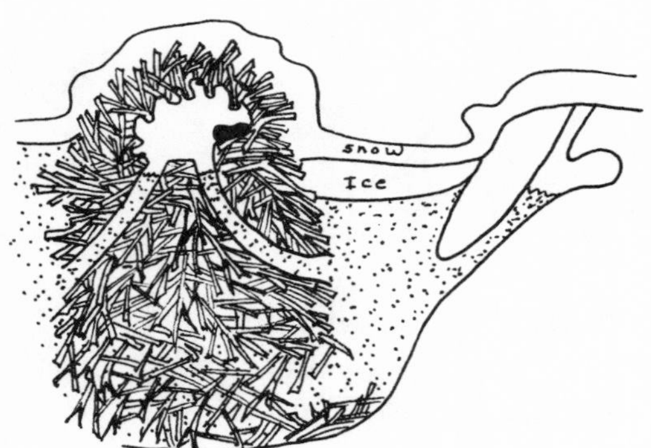

TOUGH TEETH

A beaver's front teeth are bright orange because of their super-hard enamel coat. These teeth have to be hard and sharp because the beaver uses them to cut down trees.

The back of these front teeth are softer dentine. As the beaver chews, the back wears down faster than the front of the tooth. This makes the tooth chisel-shaped.

The beaver's teeth never wear out no matter how much wood he chomps because they never stop growing.

Beavers are winter-safe unless their deep water entrance freezes shut. Then the beaver family is forced to eat its house to keep from starving to death.

RIDDLE

What did the beaver say to the tree?

ANSWER:

Caribou

CARIBOU live on the open tundra (semi-frozen plains) of Alaska and Canada. As winter approaches, thawing and refreezing of the snow covering their grazing land coats the ground with a crust of ice. It takes a lot of hoof-stomping and scraping to break through this covering. So the caribou head for the forests.

Here, the snow may be deeper, but it remains fluffy. The caribou can easily reach food, lichens and sedges. The females and young dine at the forest edge while the stronger males move into the deeper snow in the middle of the forest.

Wolverines

WOLVERINES are bad-tempered loners. They are sometimes called skunk bears because they look something like a small bear and stink like a skunk. Equipped with a heavy coat and stiff hairs on the soles of their feet, the wolverines aren't bothered by cold weather. Besides, they enjoy eating too much to hibernate.

Strong and extremely fierce, wolverines attack savagely. They have been known to drive bears and mountain lions away from a meal that they wanted for themselves.

Polar Bears

POLAR BEARS usually only take long naps during blizzards. Adult females spend five to six months dozing during the birth and early development of their cubs.

The female chooses an area on the side of a hill where snow drifts. Then she digs a long tunnel into the snow and hollows out two oval rooms. Here the air will remain as much as 40° warmer than the outside temperature. The female's breath and body heat melt enough of the snow to keep a small air hole open to the surface.

Musk Oxen

THIS IS one of the hardiest herd animals in the world. Musk oxen are built and upholstered for life in the cold North.

Looking something like a small buffalo, musk oxen have the longest hair of any North American animal. This shaggy coat may be more than 60 centimeters (24 inches) long. Its broad, sharp hoofs spread with each step. Musk oxen can run very fast across ice-crusted snow.

For defense, males and females have massive horns. The bulls form a circle around the cows and the calves facing any predator. This works well against any enemy except men with rifles.

Egg on Ice

THE EMPEROR penguin is the only penguin to breed during the Antarctic winter (in June). Female penguins lay one egg on the ice. Then the male does the incubating, holding the egg on top of his feet and allowing his abdomen to sag over the egg.

The female travels as far as 160 kilometers (100 miles) to hunt in the open sea. While she's gone, the chick hatches, and the male feeds it from a secretion produced in his crop (a food-storage organ). When the female returns to feed the young, the male goes hunting. Later, when the chick is big enough, the whole family treks to the sea.

Tracking Down Tracks

EVEN IF you don't see any animals outside in the winter, you can probably find signs that wildlife is around. Snow and bare ground show tracks clearly. From these tracks you can tell what kind of animal traveled your way, how the animal was moving, and if the animal met any other travelers.

Here are some common animal tracks to help you identify the ones you find.

Cottontail Rabbit

THE FRONT PAWS go down first and then the hind feet jump to land in front.

RIDDLE

How can you spell rabbit without using the letter R?

ANSWER: 

Running

Opposum

OPPOSUM tracks show the animal's flat-footed waddle. In the snow, you'll also see the track of the opposum's dragging tail.

Skunk

WHEN walking, the footprints may sometimes overlap.

Running

Sparrow

SPARROWS are perching birds. The side toes are not widely spread. The prints are grouped in pairs to show that the bird moves by hopping when it's on the ground. Starlings and crows walk, so their tracks are single file.

Pigeon

PIGEONS do more walking than perching so side toes are widely spread. You may find wing marks on the snow, showing where the bird took to the air.

House Cat

WALKING PRINTS are about 12.5 to 20 centimeters (5 to 8 inches) apart. Running sets of prints are about 75 centimeters (30 inches) apart.

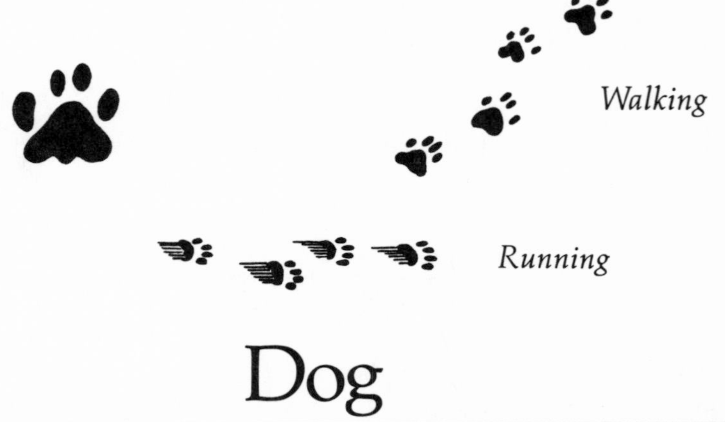

Dog

THE PRINT SIZE varies with the size of the dog as does the distance between walking prints. Running prints spread out even more. Dog prints always show claw marks and are blurred because dogs drag their toes.

Rat

THE RAT'S front feet are four-fingered hands. When sitting or crouching, the back legs are pulled up putting the hind footprints ahead of the front footprints. The line between the tracks was made by the animal's dragging tail.

Keep on Tracking

LOOK FOR an area where the snow is unmarked to check your own tracks. Take four regular steps. Then take a close look at your track. Is there anything special about your footprint (marks from your boots, shape, spacing) that could help you recognize your own track? About how far apart are your footprints?

Now, run, hop and skip across the snow. Notice how each of these methods of locomotion changed your tracks.

Go looking for other people tracks. Can you tell how each person was moving? Can you tell if the tracks were made by a man, a woman, a boy or a girl?

Collecting Tracks

IF YOU FIND tracks on bare ground, you may want to make a casting of the print to take home. Cut rings from plastic soft drink bottles or milk jugs to take with you. The sides of the rings should be about 5 centimeters (2 inches) high. You'll also need plaster of paris powder, a jug or canteen of water, and an empty soup can.

When you find a clear track, place a ring around it. Pick the track clean of pebbles, pine needles or other debris.

Fill the can half full of plaster powder and add enough water to make the mixture as thick as pancake batter. Stir with a stick until it's smooth.

Pour the plaster into the track, filling the ring almost to the top. Let the plaster harden for thirty minutes. Then lift the ring and plaster gently.

At home, let the plaster harden overnight. Peel off the ring and brush the mold clean with an old toothbrush.

Try to identify what animal made the track. Label the cast and make a display of your collection.

Snow Snakes

INDIAN TRIBES around the Great Lakes liked winter outdoor games. One of the most popular was snow snakes.

The snakes were hand-carved sticks about 3 meters (10 feet) long. Trench tracks were carefully prepared before any contest to make them as slick as possible. One story tells of a warrior who hurled his snake over a kilometer.

If you live where it snows, you can make snow snakes and have a contest of your own. For each snake, you'll need a piece of quarter round molding (available at a lumber yard) about 1.2 meters (4 feet) long.

Let the round side be the snake's belly. Taper the head end and trim off the tail. Whittle or plane the snake's back flat (you may need help with this). Then sand the snake smooth and rub on paste wax to make it fast.

Finally, add two screws and nuts as shown in the picture. These look like eyes, but they are really to add weight to the snake's front end.

To make the trench, tie a rope on a log and pull it through the snow. Be careful to make the trench straight. Pack down the sides. Choose a way to mark the distance each snake travels. For best results, slide, don't throw, your snake.

If you don't have much yard space, play this game on a playground or a parking lot. Or you could make much shorter snakes for a mini-contest.

Bug Hunt

OF THE MORE than six-hundred thousand known types of insects, only a very few are active during the winter months. Most adult bugs die leaving their eggs or developing larva (young) in a weatherproof case. A few hibernate, sleeping the winter away beneath a blanket of loose bark or tucked snugly in a dry hole. A few others, such as monarch butterflies, head south for a vacation. The few winter-lovers are a wild bunch worth looking for. January, February and early March are the best months to find these insects.

LET'S SPLIT

Picture what it would be like to have your skeleton outside your skin. If you kept growing bigger, your skeleton would become too tight. This is what happens to insects. When its exoskeleton splits open along the back, the bug crawls out. A new exoskeleton hardens over the soft skin. This process is called *molting.*

Snowfly

THE BEST KNOWN winter bug is the snowfly (also called the stonefly). They can be found along the banks of swift-flowing streams. The young crawl out of the water onto the ice and snow. Then they molt once more to become adults.

During their short adulthood, snowflies eat the algae that grows on the snow. After mating, the females go back to the icy water to lay their eggs.

These insects have complete metamorphosis (see page 108).

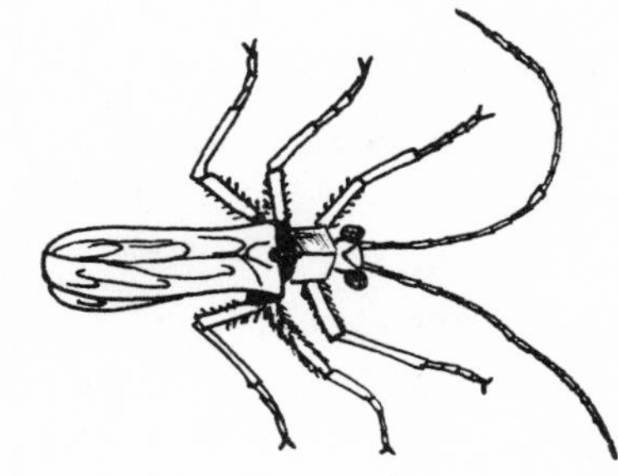

Length: 1 centimeter (.4 inch) or less

COMPLETE METAMORPHOSIS

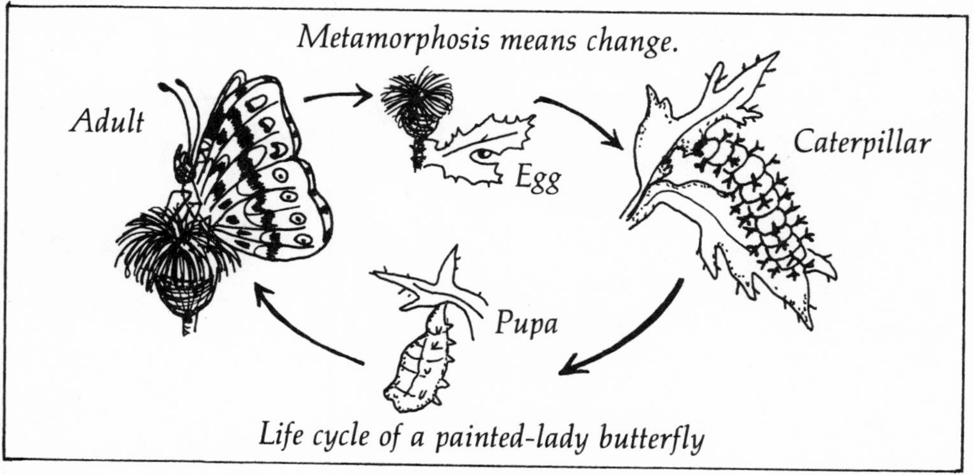

Life cycle of a painted-lady butterfly

True Bugs

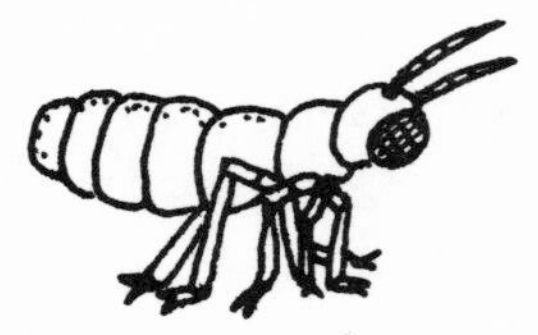

Some invertebrates (animals without backbones) mimic insects, but to be a real member of the bug family the critter must have:

1. A body with 3 clearly defined regions—head, thorax, abdomen.
2. An exoskeleton.
3. A head with 6 segments, 2 antennae, compound and simple eyes, and mouth parts designed for chewing, sucking or lapping.
4. 6 legs.
5. Breathing tubes that connect to spiracles (tiny holes on the abdomen).
6. A body temperature that changes with the air temperature (cold-blooded).

Springtails

ALSO CALLED snow fleas, these tiny insects leap around on snowbanks. Their bounce is due to two spines folded forward on the underside of their abdomen.

Springtails have no metamorphosis. This means that the young look exactly like their parents—only smaller. They eat sap which oozes from trees or decaying plants.

Fossil springtails have been found on rocks 300 million years old. The fossil bugs look just like the ones you can see today.

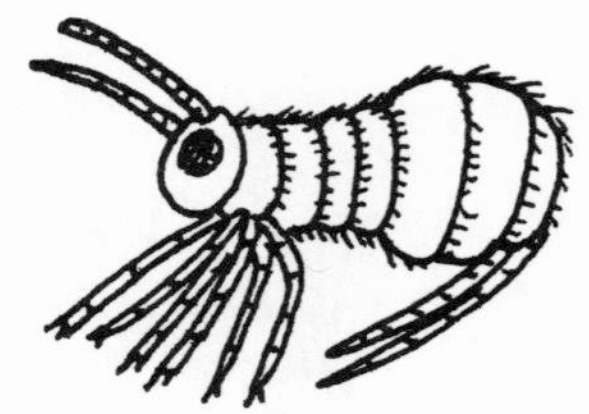

Length: 2 millemeters (.08 inches)

Scorpionflies

SCORPIONFLIES got their name because the males curl up their slender abdomen as they run. Males and females have trunklike snouts with the mouthparts at the tip. The young develop in the moss or decaying leaves buried under the snow.

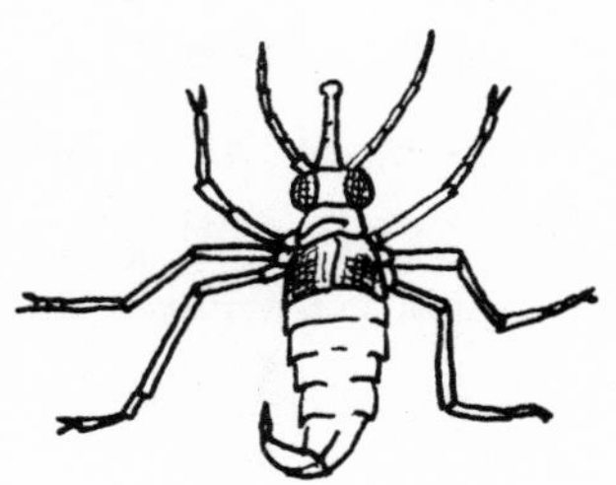

Length: 2-5 millimeters (.08-.2 inches)

Winter Crane Flies

WINTER CRANE flies look a lot like mosquitoes, but they don't have wings. They spend their entire lives in their snowy homes. The adults crawl up through the snow to mate. Then they crawl back into the cold snowbank. The females lay their eggs in piles of leaves under the snow. The larvae feed on the decaying plant matter.

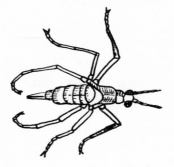

Length: 1 centimeter (.4 inches)

RIDDLE

Why is snow like a tree?

ANSWER:

Winter Zoo

GO HUNTING AGAIN, but this time take along a supply of resealable plastic bags. Look for cocoons and egg cases. Search inside dried curled leaves, on branches, and under loose bark. Turn over stones and old logs. Examine window ledges, fence posts, and protected places around your house's foundation.

When you find a cocoon or egg case, handle it with care. Rough treatment could hurt the animals inside.

When you get home, put each cocoon or egg case into a separate jar. Cover the jar with a lid that has several small holes in it or with a piece of gauze secured by a rubber band. This will allow air to circulate while keeping your collection caged.

Keep your winter zoo outside. The eggs and larvae need to be in the cold to continue their life cycle. If you take them inside, the larvae will dry out and die. The eggs will hatch before there is food available for the young animals.

When spring comes, watch what comes out of the cocoons or eggs. Then turn the animals loose.

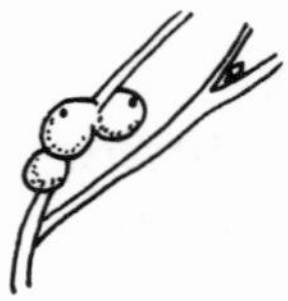

A gall is a bump on a twig or a leaf. Inside, there is a larvae waiting for spring.

A hard, frothy brown case is a mantis egg case.

A bagworm's egg basket looks like dead leaves.

Bring 'Em Home Alive

WHEN you're collecting cocoons, you want ones with live young inside. But how can you tell which cocoons have living pupae?

1. Lift it. A cocoon with a live pupa is heavier than one with a dead pupa or one that is empty.
2. Shake *gently*. A live pupa will make a dull thump as it hits the inside walls of the cocoon. A rattle means an empty cocoon with a dry pupa skin left inside.
3. Look for holes. If the hole is big, the cocoon is an old one and the pupa has already changed and left as an adult. If the hole is tiny, and *ichneumon wasp* has probably laid her eggs inside. This means the young wasps have killed the pupa.
4. Hold it up to the light. If the cocoon is thin, you'll be able to see inside. Do you see a pupa?

WHOSE COCOON IS IT?

Adult Moth	Cocoon	Range	Where To Look
Polyphemus		Throughout U.S.	On the ground under trees or on twigs
Cecropia		Atlantic coast to Rockies	On trees and shrubs
White masked Tussock Moth		Eastern U.S. to Colorado	On tree trunks, fence posts and similar places
Luna		Eastern U.S. to Great Plains	Among leaves on the ground near trees

Use books to help you identify other cocoons.

Don't Swallow That Pill!

SOWBUGS are also called pillbugs because when disturbed they curl up into a tight, round pill shape. Pillbugs hibernate in the winter, but you can find them under rocks or under piles of dead leaves close to the foundation of a house.

Put your bugs in a jar or a bag and take them home for this investigation.

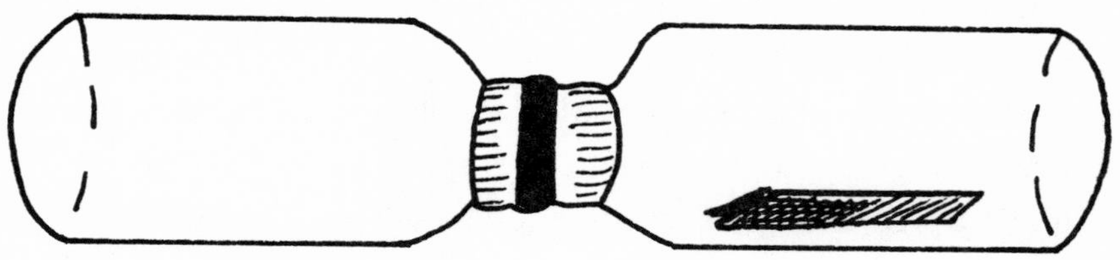

Use electrician's tape to attach two screw-on-metal-ring canning jar lids together at the top. Put a damp paper towel into one quart jar and screw it onto one of the ring lids. Put the sowbugs into another jar and screw it onto the second ring lid.

Now, the jars are connected by a ring-top bridge. As the hibernating bugs begin to warm up, they will uncurl and start to explore their new environment.

Do they prefer the dry jar or do they move into the jar with the damp towel? Think of a way you could find out if pillbugs like light or dark places best.

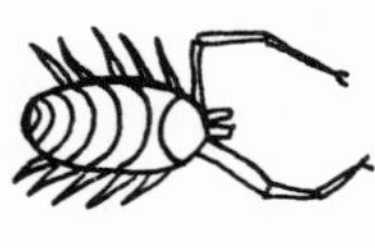

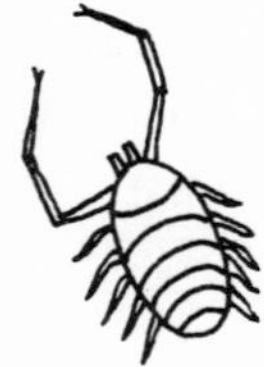

OFF AND RUNNING

Hold a Pillbug Derby. Each person will need a bug racer, a sheet of paper, and a pencil. A starting X is drawn on each paper. At a signal, the pillbugs are placed on the marks.

The bugs are off!

An official timer clocks one minute while each person tracks their racer with a pencil line. No fair prodding the pillbugs.

When the time is up, a judge measures the trails. The pillbug that traveled the farthest is the champ. When all the races are over, return the bugs to the shelter of the rock or leaves where you found them.

Hidden Life

WHILE you're discovering winter wildlife, take a close look at the trees. The branches and twigs aren't bare, and they aren't dead. The trees are studded with buds and full of life.

The buds you've found began growing last spring and matured during the summer. Now, wearing a weatherproof coat, these winter buds hold next year's growth. That's right—branches, leaves, and flowers.

Hard to believe? Carefully peel open a large end bud. You'll find a tiny, soft, green twig twisted and folded inside along with supersmall leaves and flowers.

Because each tree's winter buds look different, you can use them to identify types of trees. A winter twig collection makes an attractive and interesting display.

Ring Around the Twig

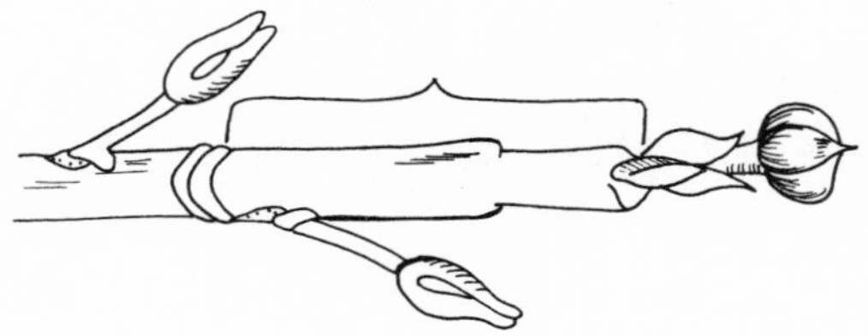

RINGS around a twig aren't dirt. They're growth lines. To find out how much a twig grew last year, first find the terminal bud (at the very end of the twig). Then look along the twig until you find the first set of rings. This is the location of last year's terminal bud.

The distance between the rings and the terminal bud is the growth for last year. Count how many groups of rings you see on the twig and you'll know how old the twig is.

INSIDE RINGS

Find a tree stump and take a close look at those rings. Every year a tree produces a light-colored ring of spring growth and a dark-colored ring of summer growth.

If you count either the light or the dark rings (not both), you'll be able to tell how old the tree was when it died or was cut.

RIDDLE

What wears a covering in the summer and goes bare in the winter?

ANSWER:

A Twig and Its Parts

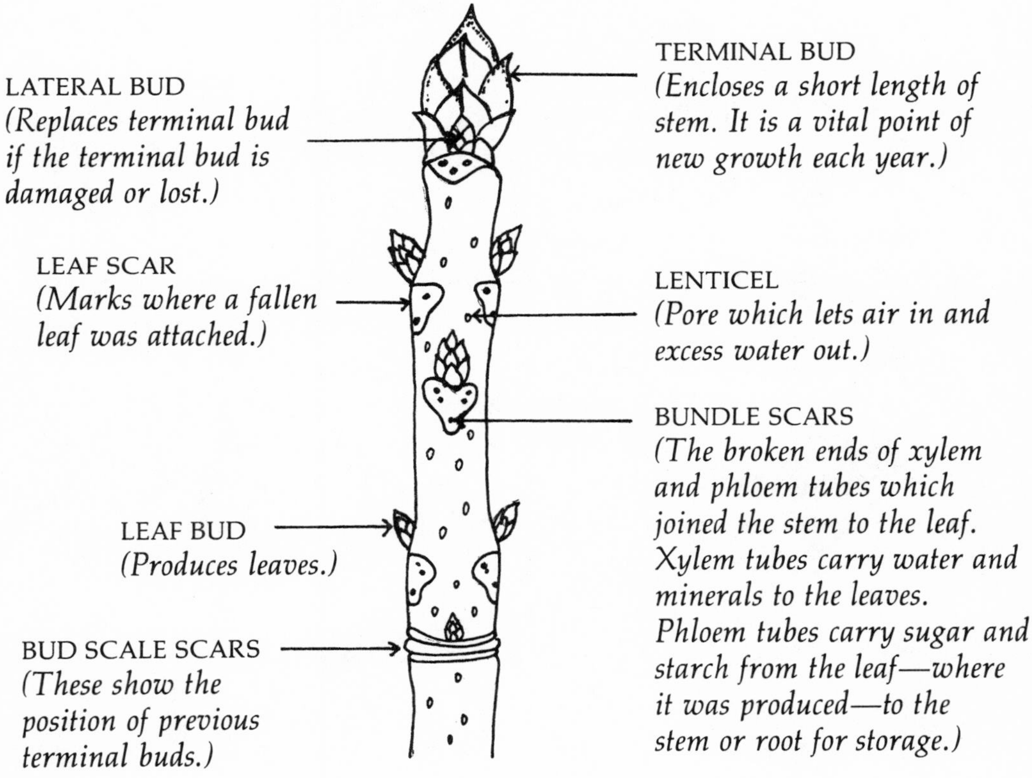

LATERAL BUD
(Replaces terminal bud if the terminal bud is damaged or lost.)
TERMINAL BUD
(Encloses a short length of stem. It is a vital point of new growth each year.)
LEAF SCAR
(Marks where a fallen leaf was attached.)
LENTICEL
(Pore which lets air in and excess water out.)
BUNDLE SCARS
(The broken ends of xylem and phloem tubes which joined the stem to the leaf. Xylem tubes carry water and minerals to the leaves. Phloem tubes carry sugar and starch from the leaf—where it was produced—to the stem or root for storage.)
LEAF BUD
(Produces leaves.)
BUD SCALE SCARS
(These show the position of previous terminal buds.)

Three Patterns of Bud Arrangement on a Twig

Opposite MAPLE — *Alternate* BIRCH — *Whorled* CATALPA

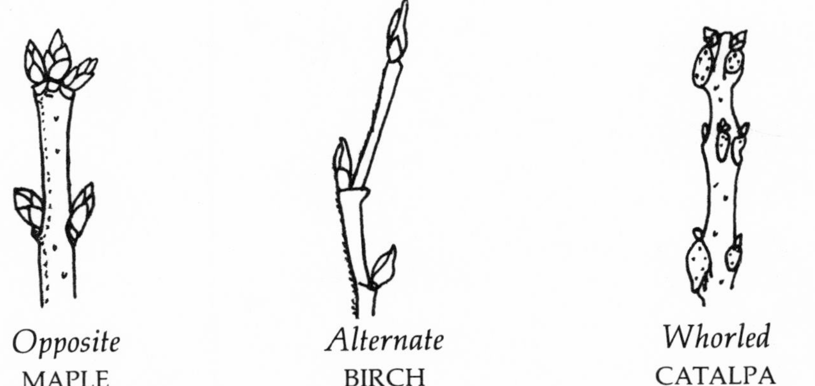

Putting your Collection Together

WHEN YOU collect the twigs, always choose ones with a terminal bud. Many times the terminal bud is different from the leaf buds, and it's needed for identification. Break off twigs that are about 15 centimeters (6 inches) long.

At home, measure your twigs and use a pocket knife to shorten any that are too long. Slice off the end of each twig at a slant so the inside is visible.

Use 5x7 index cards to mount your collection (one to a card). These pictures of twigs from some of the most common trees will help you identify your collection. For further help check books of winter twigs and books about trees.

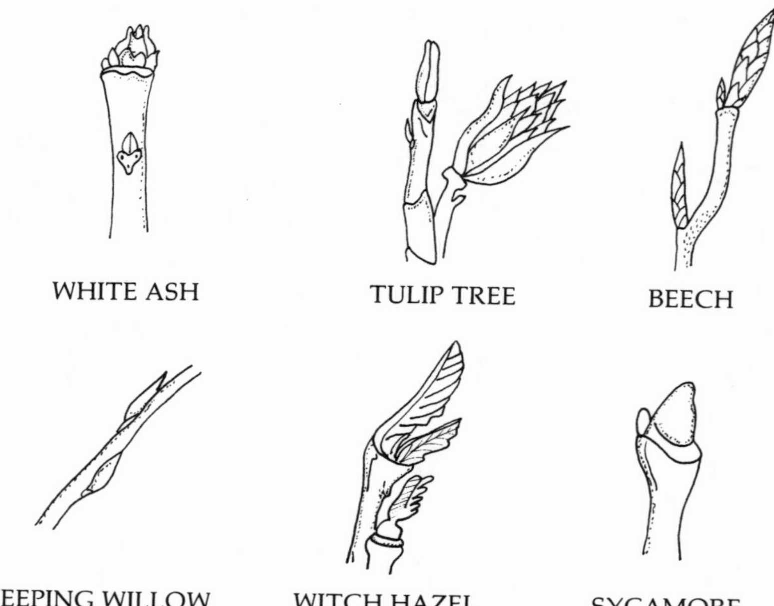

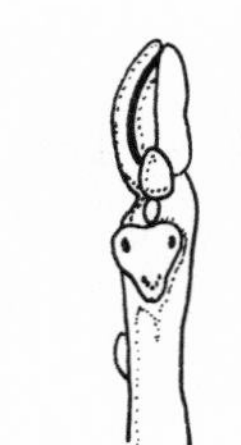

BUTTERNUT

BLACK WALNUT

BLACK MAPLE

SUGAR MAPLE

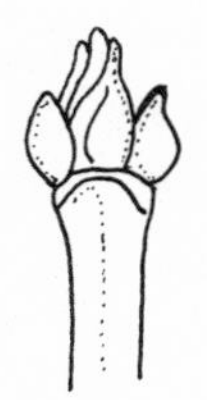

BOXELDER

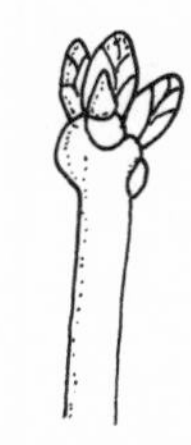

SCARLET OAK

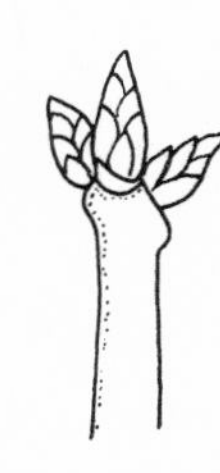

BLACK OAK

APPLE

EARLY BLOOMERS

You can cut twigs or branches from flowering bushes such as pussy willow or forsythia and bring them inside for early blooms.

There must have been four to six weeks with temperatures below 3°C. (37°F.) before this will work.

Put the twigs or branches in a vase and partly fill it with water. Place the vase near a window where it will receive plenty of sunlight. Like magic, within a couple of days, you will be a blooming success!

You've discovered that it can be a lot of fun to explore outside in winter, but sometimes winter weather can be terrible. What can you do when the wind is making already cold temperatures dangerously cold? And what about those days when sleet is pelting the ground or a blizzard is raging? Well, when winter is too awful to go outside, stay inside and explore the next chapter.

6. UNDERCOVER EXPLORA-TIONS

Winter Gardening

MANY PLANTS are glad to grow in the summer warmth of your house. For some seeds, however, warm weather is the pits unless it's been cold first. These seeds have a built-in time clock set for a winter's nap before they start the hard job of growing.

You can coax these seeds into sprouting by giving them an artifical winter. Collect several peach pits, apple seeds and plum pits. Spread these seeds on a pie plate and put them in the refrigerator.

Let the seeds rest in the cold wintertime darkness of your refrigerator for six weeks. Turn them occasionally.

Then bring the seeds into springtime. Plant them in plastic cups filled with potting soil. Poke the seeds about 1.25 centimeters (½ inch) under the soil and sprinkle with water. Place the cups in a warm, sunny spot. Keep the soil moist. It may take several weeks before a tiny green shoot pushes out.

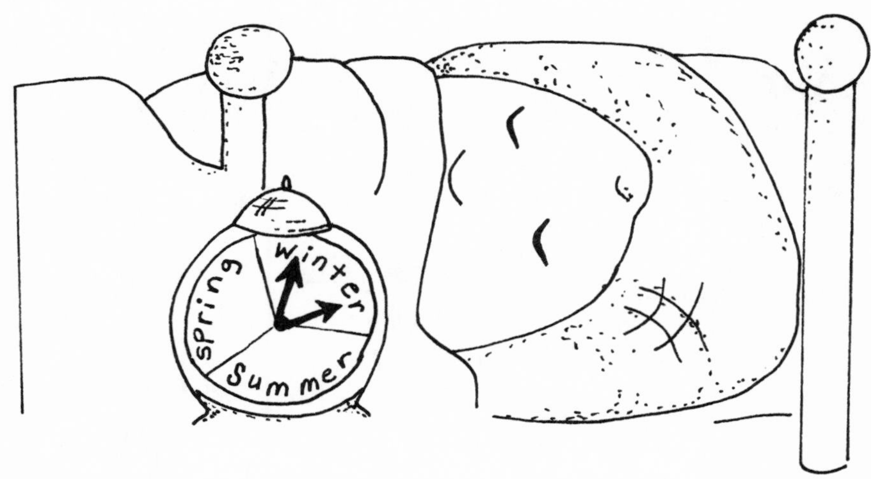

The seeds you've been feeding to the birds won't need much encouragement to sprout. Put a small handful (about two tablespoons) of seed into a bowl and cover with lukewarm water. Let the seeds sit overnight. This helps speed up sprouting.

Plant the seeds by spreading them evenly over the surface of a cupful of potting soil. Cover the seeds with a thin layer of soil. Sprinkle with water and place the cup in a warm, sunny spot.

Watch the sprouting plants. You'll discover a delightful variety. Use books to help you identify what plants are growing in your garden.

When the sprouts are about 10 centimeters (4 inches) tall, transplant them to bigger pots with good drainage. If you can keep your garden growing until after the last frost, transplant the young plants outside. You'll be able to grow your own seed to feed the birds next winter.

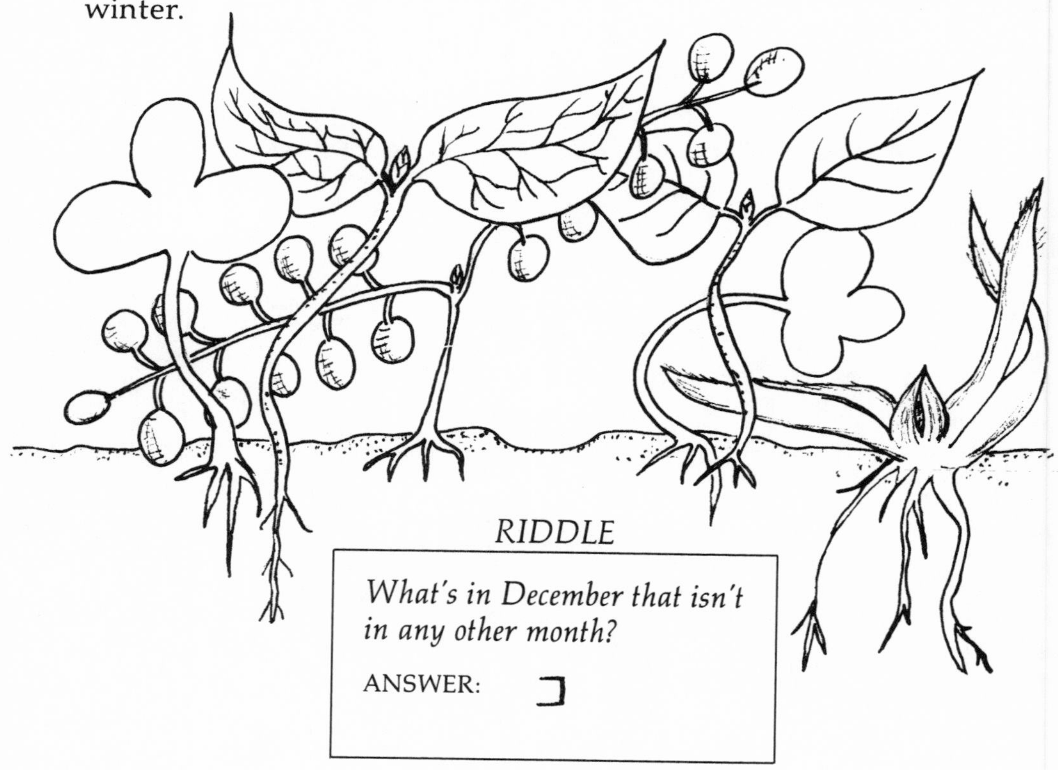

RIDDLE
What's in December that isn't in any other month?
ANSWER:

A Garden You Can Eat

BUY DRY mung beans, dry soy beans or alfalfa seeds at a health food store. Cover the bottom of a glass dish or glass pie plate with beans. Pour lukewarm water over the seeds and let them sit overnight.

After you've drained off the water, lay a damp paper towel in the dish and arrange the seeds on the towel. They should not be on top of each other. Cover the dish with clear plastic wrap and put it in a shady, warm spot.

The seeds will sprout quickly. Within three days the sprouts should be big enough to eat.

Toss the sprouts with lettuce. Add crumbled cheese and your favorite dressing. This garden makes a fresh and tasty salad.

Sprout a Spud *(Not to Eat)*

A SWEET POTATO is nice for this project because it produces an attractive, leafy vine. But any type of potato will do.

Choose a container that's deep enough that part of the potato can be underwater without resting on the bottom. If necessary, use toothpicks to support the spud. Keep the container in a sunny place and add water as needed. Part of the potato must remain underwater for it to sprout. Keeping the entire potato underwater will give you *rotten* results.

Popcorn

(Easy to Keep, Good to Eat)

BEFORE REFRIGERATORS and freezers, the main ways of storing food for winter were canning and drying. Popcorn is a native American plant, and the Indians were drying it for winter eating long before any white settlers arrived. But the varieties of popcorn that the Indians grew were very different from the ones you can buy in grocery stores today.

In one variety, the kernels stayed attached to the strands of silk when they popped. That kind of popcorn was used to make ceremonial headdresses and ornaments. Christopher Columbus was given a popcorn corsage by the Indians of San Salvador in 1492. Another variety popped but remained on the cob. Imagine sinking your teeth into popcorn on the cob. Popcorn was one of the gifts the Indians brought the Pilgrims at the first Thanksgiving feast.

BREAKFAST FOR PILGRIMS

You can try the original puffed breakfast cereal. Pop some corn. Put the popped corn in a bowl and pour on milk. This was a favorite morning meal for the Pilgrims.

POPCORN LOVERS

Every man, woman and child in the U.S. can be counted on to eat an average of .9 kilograms (2 pounds) of popcorn every year. People in the Midwest usually eat more than the average, and people in Milwaukee, Minneapolis/St. Paul, Chicago and Seattle are the popcorn-eating champs. These folks munch an average 1.8 kilograms (4 pounds) of popcorn a year.

Today's popcorn varieties are all hybrids—developed by crossing two different kinds of popcorn plants. In an attempt to grow the perfect popcorn, over thirty-thousand new hybrids are grown every year. Some like Burpee's peppy corn, creme-puff, white cloud, tom thumb and gourmet are good enough for farmers to produce for market. Most, like the snowpuff variety, are popcorn freaks. Only two or three popped kernels of snowpuff popcorn would fill a bowl. But the popped snowpuff kernels aren't very tasty. Good popcorn must taste good, expand well (thirty to thirty four times its original size is considered good), and be counted on to pop.

Popping Up a Batch

ARE YOU ready to pop up a treat for yourself? Collect a four quart pan with a lid, oil (margarine and butter burn) and some popcorn.

1. Pour three tablespoons of oil into the pan. Add one kernel and heat on medium-high until the kernel pops.
2. Add one-half cup popcorn. Put the lid on loosely and shake gently.

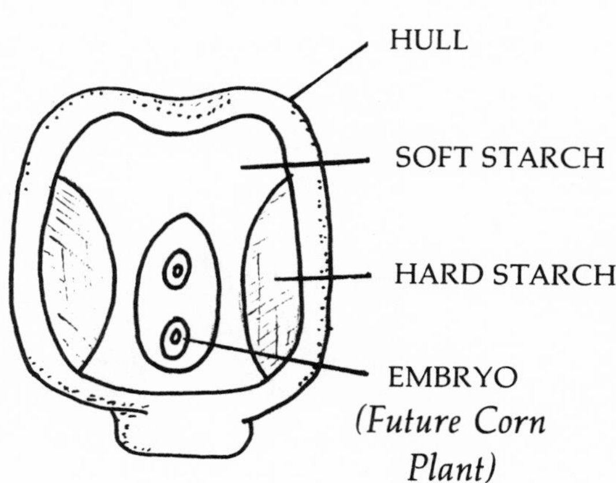

Inside the hard seed coat and hard starch layer is a moist, soft pulp. Popcorn needs to be around 200°C./400°F. to pop. The oil and shaking help to spread the heat evenly around the kernels. The moisture inside the kernel turns to steam but is held in by the hard starch and seed coat. The soft pulp swells until . . . POP! The hard shell bursts open and the kernel turns inside out.

The loose-fitting lid lets the steam out so the popcorn doesn't become soggy. After the corn is popped, you may want to add melted butter, seasonings and salt. Never add salt before the corn is popped. This makes the popcorn tough.

Some Tasty Additions

ADD THESE to one batch (four quarts) of popped corn.

Chili-Cheese: Sprinkle on one-half teaspoon of chili powder. Toss. Then add one cup of grated American cheese. Spread the popped corn on a cookie sheet and put it in the oven. Heat at 325° until the cheese melts.

Sweet Treat: Stir together one-half cup apple jelly and one-fourth cup honey. Heat in a saucepan until the mixture is runny. Pour the apple-honey over the popped corn. Mix gently until all the kernels are coated.

Corny Jewelry

POPCORN JEWELRY was a favorite with the Indians. You can make some popcorn jewelry of your own.

Pop some corn (don't butter it). Thread dental floss on a needle. Then string on the popcorn by poking the needle through the thickest part of the popped kernel.

String enough for a necklace or a bracelet. Leave some string to tie into a knot. Trim off the extra floss.

When you're tired of wearing your popcorn jewelry, hang it outside on a tree as a treat for the birds.

Putting Back The Pop

IF YOUR POPCORN has a lot of duds (unpopped kernels), it is probably too dry. The soft pulpy center must contain thirteen to fourteen percent moisture to pop successfully. To put the pop back, fill a quart jar nearly full of kernels. Add two tablespoons of water. Screw a lid tightly on the jar and shake to distribute the water. Let the popcorn sit overnight.

The next batch you whip up should pop much more successfully.

Apple Leather

THIS IS an old time candy that you can make to enjoy and to share with friends when you're stuck inside on a winter day.

Combine three cups of apple sauce with one-half cup sugar and one-fourth teaspoon cinnamon. Spread this mixture on a jellyroll pan (or a cookie sheet). Bake at 200° for four to six hours (until it becomes leathery).

Remove from the oven and sprinkle with powdered sugar. Let the apple leather cool. Then peel it out of the pan and cut it into thin slices. Munch on this while you try some other investigations and activities.

PIT TOSS

This was a favorite Crow Indian game. It could easily be played while huddling around the fire.

Collect six peach pits for playing pieces. Use a marking pen to color a stripe across the middle of one side of each pit.

Play this game with your friends. Divide into two teams. Any number can play as long as the teams are equal. Put the pits into a small bowl.

Each player in turn holds the bowl, flips the pits into the air, and catches them again. Dropped pits don't count. One point is scored for each striped pit. Play alternates between the teams.

Players keep their own scores. Team totals are added up after each player has made twenty tosses. The team with the most points wins.

Make Some Frost

IN THIS investigation you can watch frost form and end up with a delicious ice cream snack.

You'll need: one pint of half and half, one can of evaporated milk, one cup of granulated sugar, four eggs, two teaspoons of vanilla, one gallon of whole milk, a four- to six-quart ice cream freezer, a box of rock salt, and a bag of crushed ice.

Break the eggs into a large mixing bowl. Beat until the eggs are frothy. Add the half and half, the evaporated milk, the sugar, and the vanilla. Beat the mixture for two minutes.

Pour the ice cream mix into the ice cream bucket. Add enough milk to bring the solution up to the fill line. Stir until well blended.

Put in the dasher and close the freezer can. Layer the bucket around the can with crushed ice and sprinkles of rock salt until the ice is about 2.5 centimeters (1 inch) below the can lid. Freeze by following the manufacturer's directions.

Watch for frost to begin to form on the outside of the can. Then look at the frost patterns through a magnifying glass.

Are all the crystals the same size? Do any of the crystals overlap? What shape are the crystals?

When the ice cream is firm, open the can and dig in.

A Short History of Ice Cream

Ice cream evolved from the iced wines and fruit juices of ancient times. The Roman emperor Nero had runners bring ice and snow from mountain areas to make these special cold treats.

In the thirteenth century, Marco Polo brought recipes for water ices to Italy from the Orient. Ice cream was introduced to America in 1600 by the English colonists.

The invention of the hand-crank freezer in 1846 made it possible for people to make their own ice cream at home.

Ice On a String

DID YOU wonder why you added rock salt to the ice to speed the freezing process?

The answer is that salt water freezes at a lower temperature than fresh water. When salt is sprinkled on ice, the ice begins to melt. The heat needed to melt the ice is drawn from the material the ice is touching. In this case, the heat is drawn from the freezer can, and the ice cream mixture becomes colder.

Here's another investigation that will show you this process in action.

Fill a glass nearly full of water and float an ice cube in the water. Use a piece of thread about 20 to 25 centimeters (8 to 10 inches) long. Dip one end in the water and coil about 5 centimeters (2 inches) of this wet end on top of the cube. Sprinkle salt over the top of the cube and the thread.

Wait about one minute and then pull on the thread. Surprise! The ice cube will lift with the thread.

The salt melted the surface of the ice cube. To melt, the ice took heat from the wet thread. Enough heat was removed to make the water on the thread freeze. This glaze of ice made the thread stick to the ice cube.

RIDDLE

What do you call Eskimo cows?

ANSWER:

Is the weather still bad? Well, here are some ways the Eskimos spend the long, dark Arctic days when it's too terrible to go outside.

Buzzer

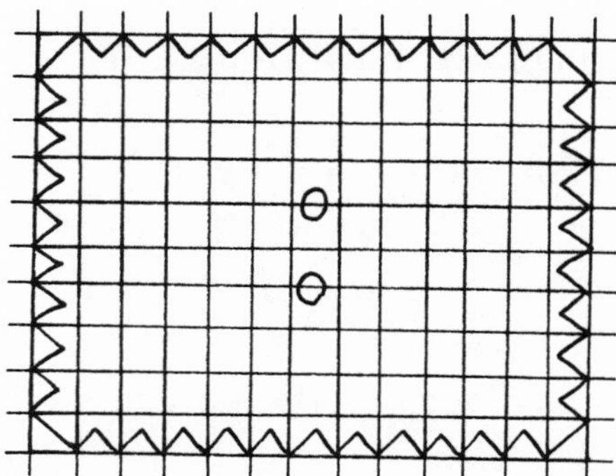

COPY THIS pattern of a buzzer on paper lined with 7 millimeter (¼ inch) squares—such as graph paper. Draw the design using thirteen squares across and ten squares down. Tape the pattern on a piece of plywood 62.5 X 87.5 X 7 millimeters (2½ X 3½ X ¼ inches).

You may want to have an adult help you cut around the pattern with a coping saw. Make the notches even. Drill one small hole above and below the exact center of the board.

Sand the wood smooth. Then collect 100 centimeters (40 inches) of string or cord. Make sure it fits easily through the holes in the buzzer. Thread it through the holes and tie the ends into a tight knot. Cut off any extra string.

Hold one end of the looped string in each hand. Pull the string tight. Then move your hands closer together to relax the string. Suddenly, snap the string tight again.

Pull and release, pull and release. As the buzzer spins it makes a noise. The faster it spins, the louder it buzzes.

Smooth it Away

ESKIMO SCULPTURES are usually carved with a knife from a heavy, fairly soft stone called *steatite* (also called soapstone). These sculptures are simple and show animals or people familiar to the Eskimos.

You can make an Eskimo-style sculpture using plaster of Paris or a bar of fairly soft soap and a pocketknife. You'll need medium-rough sandpaper with the plaster and a damp paper towel with the soap.

If you're using plaster of Paris, clean out a half pint milk carton and open the top. Mix two cups of the powder with enough water to make the plaster as thick as pancake batter. Stir until the plaster is smooth. Then pour it into the carton. Let the plaster sit until it's completely dry and hard (about twenty-four hours).

Choose a design for your sculpture. Keep the design very simple. Peel off the carton and draw your design on the plaster block. Or draw your design on the bar of soap.

Think about which sections should be cut lower. Carve these away. Finish by smoothing the edges. Use the sandpaper to smooth the plaster sculpture. Smooth the soap with the damp paper towel.

Bull Roarer

THIS NOISEMAKER was popular with a number of Indian tribes besides the Eskimos. In some tribes, it was more than a toy. The medicine man used it to call the wind or to ward off evil spirits.

Collect a paint stirring stick from a paint dealer or a hardware store (they're free or very inexpensive). Sand the wood smooth and drill a hole in the base (as shown on the pattern). You may want to paint a design on the wood. The Indians thought that pictures helped the magic.

Cut a piece of string about 50 centimeters (20 inches) long. Put one end through the hole and tie a knot so the string can't pull out. Tie the other end to a stick or a short piece of wood dowel. To keep the string from slipping off the handle, carve a groove in the handle with a pocketknife. Fit the string into this groove.

Grasp the handle in one hand and spin the bull roarer over your head. The faster you swing it, the louder it will roar.

Sap's Running

ARE THE DAYS getting longer? Are thawing days alternating with freezing nights? Have you seen squirrels nipping at tender twigs on sugar maple trees?

These are signs that the sap is starting to flow. And when the sap starts, spring is coming. Maple sugar is the first harvest of the year.

Early settlers learned the trick of collecting this sweet sap from the Indians. The Indians sometimes killed the trees with their crude methods of tapping. They broke off branches, chopped open the wood, or tore off large chunks of bark. Later, the Indians learned to "box" the trees, cutting a square hole and hollowing out a bowl-shaped place in the wood for the sap to collect.

A wood-chip spout directed the sap into a birch bark bucket.

Cooking down the sap was a long slow process. The sap had to be boiled until the water was mostly gone. Since the Indians only had bark pots, they couldn't boil the sap directly over the fire. Stones had to be heated and dropped into the pots. Then the stones had to be lifted out and reheated.

The settlers improved on this

process by using metal kettles. But boiling the sap until it thickened still took many hours.

Different Kinds of Maple Sugar *(All of Them Good)*

STIRRED SUGAR	Boiled, scraped and stirred until it is grainy and almost dry. This can be stored for a long time and is used in cooking.
CAKE OR BLOCK SUGAR	Boiled until the syrup is very thick. Then the syrup is poured into molds and allowed to harden. Cake sugar is sometimes molded into shapes such as moons, flowers, and maple leaves.
MAPLE SYRUP	Boiled until the liquid "aprons off" (falls in a sheet from a ladle).

Sap Facts

SAP CONTAINS mostly water. Only one to twelve per cent of sap is sugar.

Sap flows best on a bright sunny morning after a cold clear night. Sap flows really well when the temperature is about 4°C. (40°F.).

It takes thirty to thirty-five gallons of sap to produce one gallon of syrup.

The average sugar maple tree yields ten to twelve gallons of sap per taphole each season.

Sap stops flowing if the temperature falls and stays below -1°C. (30°F.) or if the temperature rises above 10°C. (50°F.). Sap stops flowing for the year once the buds burst open (usually in April).

Wax Sugar

ORIGINALLY, wax sugar was made by dropping hot syrup onto snow. You can try this taste treat. Heat some maple syrup (use the real thing). Drizzle it onto a scoop of crushed ice. Pick off the strands of sticky maple taffy with your fingers.

BUDDY RUN

The sap that runs after the buds begin to swell has a leathery taste. It doesn't make good syrup.

The End *(for this year)*

ONCE THE BUDS burst open on the sugar maples, winter is over. Oh, there may still be a late snowstorm, but the ground won't stay covered for long. Green shoots are pushing up, and animals that have been sleeping are waking up. Migrating animals are also starting to return.

There will be a lot of new things for you to do, but winter exploring—that cold, nose-nipping fun—is over.

You'll have to wait until the next time it's winter to try those icy investigations and go winter exploring again.

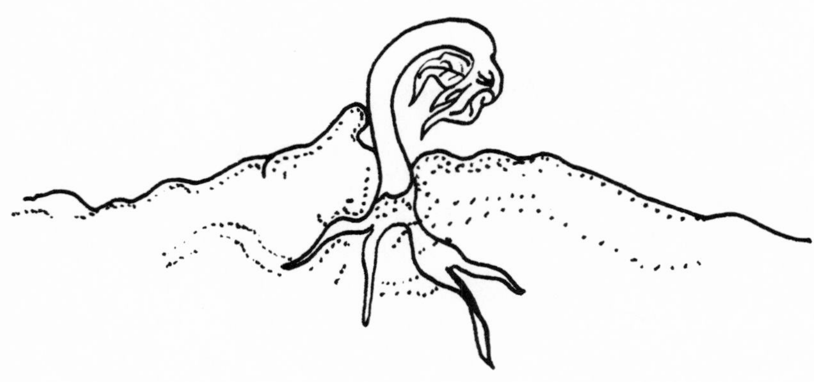

Riddle Answers

PAGE	
24	The river bank
31	Heat, because you can catch cold
41	Justice (just ice)
42	Wind
46	Pepper
51	Because there is a night in between
58	Arctic circles
69	Snow
85	Star warts
85	The ice might crack up
87	A copsicle
94	In snowbanks
108	Because it's kept on ice
110	It's been nice gnawing you
116	Bunny
125	Because it leaves in the spring
130	A tree
138	D
146	Eskimoos